Pope Francis

MORNING HOMILIES IV

POPE FRANCIS

MORNING HOMILIES IV

In the Chapel of St. Martha's Guest House
July 7 – November 27, 2014

ORBIS BOOKS
Maryknoll, New York 10545

Founded in 1970, Orbis Books endeavors to publish works that enlighten the mind, nourish the spirit, and challenge the conscience. The publishing arm of the Mary knoll Fathers and Brothers, Orbis seeks to explore the global dimensions of the Christian faith and mission, to invite dialogue with diverse cultures and religious traditions, and to serve the cause of reconciliation and peace. The books published reflect the views of their authors and do not represent the official position of the Maryknoll Society. To learn more about Maryknoll and Orbis Books, please visit our website at www.maryknollsociety.org.

Library of Congress Cataloging in Publication
Francis, Pope, 1936-
  [Sermons. Selections. English]
  Pope Francis morning homilies : in the Chapel of St. Martha's guest house /vols. 1 – 3 translated by Dinah Livingstone.
    4 volumes cm
    Contents: I. 22 March–6 July 2013 II. 2 September 2013–31 January 2014 III. 3 February–30 June 2014 IV. 7 July - 27 November 2014
    ISBN 978-1-62698-111-9 (v. 1 : pbk.)
    ISBN 978-1-62698-147-8 (v. 2 : pbk.)
    ISBN 978-1-62698-179-9 (v. 3 : pbk.)
    ISBN 978-1-62698-228-4 (v. 4 : pbk.)
  1. Catholic Church—Sermons. I. Title.
BX1756.F677S4713 2015
252'.02—dc23
                                                    2014033307

Contents

Preface

Each morning Pope Francis begins his day by celebrating Mass in the chapel of Casa Santa Marta, the Vatican guest house where he has chosen to live. Those in attendance vary, including other residents and staff, curial officials, visiting dignitaries, foreign bishops, representatives of religious congregations, or others who contribute to the daily upkeep of the Vatican, such as postal workers, gardeners, and the waste collection staff. This volume of the Pope's *Morning Homilies*, the fourth in an ongoing series, is again based on the accounts published each day in *L'Osservatore Romano*. Through these accounts it is possible for those not present to experience and enjoy the Pope's lively manner of speaking and his capacity to engage his listeners and their daily lives.

We know what great significance Pope Francis attaches to preaching. In his apostolic exhortation *Evangelii Gaudium* he dedicated an entire chapter to the homily, *the touchstone for judging a pastor's closeness and ability to communicate to his people* (*EG* 125). There he provided numerous guidelines for effective preaching, noting that the homily *should be brief and avoid taking on the semblance of a speech or a lecture*; it should be positive, *not so much concerned with pointing out what shouldn't be done, but with suggesting what we can do better*; it should respect the original intent of the text (*if a text was written to console, it should not be used to correct errors*); it should avoid *abstract truths and cold syllogisms* and it should make effective use of imagery. (Here he reinforced his point by recalling the words of an old teacher, who taught him that a good homily should have an *idea, a sentiment, an im-*

age.) Above all, he likens the homily to a conversation "between a mother and child": *Even if the homily at times may be somewhat tedious, if this maternal and ecclesial spirit is present, it will always bear fruit, just as the tedious counsels of a mother bear fruit, in due time, in the hearts of her children* (140).

From his Morning Homilies at St. Martha's we can see how closely Pope Francis heeds his own advice. His homilies are certainly short and positive, filled with memorable images. They are marked throughout by his familiar themes: the importance of mercy and forgiveness, the role of Jesus as Savior, the dangerous of a church closed in on itself, the gospel as a source of life and joy.

But what is mostly striking is the intimacy and spontaneity of these homilies. Here is not the voice of a pontiff addressing the cares of the world, the universal church, or even the church of Rome, but a pastor sharing the Word of God with his immediate flock. He directs the message as much to himself as anyone else, acknowledging the same challenges, seeking the same consolation and healing.

The homily, as Pope Francis has observed, can be an *intense and happy experience of the Spirit, a consoling encounter with God's word, a constant source of renewal and growth* (*EG*, 135). May that happy experience become available to all who read this book!

—*Robert Ellsberg*

Pope Francis

MORNING HOMILIES IV

IN THE CHAPEL OF ST. MARTHA'S GUEST HOUSE

HOLY MASS WITH A GROUP OF CLERGY SEX ABUSE VICTIMS

Monday, July 7, 2014

The scene where Peter sees Jesus emerge after a terrible interrogation . . . Peter, whose eyes meet the gaze of Jesus, and weeps . . . This scene comes to my mind as I look at you, and think of so many men and women, boys and girls. I feel the gaze of Jesus and I ask for the grace to weep, the grace for the church to weep and make reparation for her sons and daughters who betrayed their mission, who abused innocent persons. Today, I am very grateful to you for having traveled so far to come here.

For some time now I have felt in my heart deep pain and suffering. So much time hidden, camouflaged with a complicity that cannot be explained until someone realized that Jesus was looking and others the same . . . and they set about to sustain that gaze.

And those few who began to weep have touched our conscience for this crime and grave sin. This is what causes me distress and pain at the fact that some priests and bishops, by sexually abusing minors, violated their innocence and their own priestly vocation. It is something more than despicable actions. It is like a sacrilegious cult, because these boys and girls had

3

been entrusted to the priestly charism in order to be brought to God. And those people sacrificed them to the idol of their own concupiscence. They profaned the very image of God in whose likeness we were created. Childhood, as we all know, is a treasure. Young hearts, so open and trusting, have their own way of understanding the mysteries of God's love and are eager to grow in the faith. Today the heart of the church looks into the eyes of Jesus in these boys and girls and wants to weep; she asks the grace to weep before the execrable acts of abuse which have left lifelong scars.

I know that these wounds are a source of deep and often unrelenting emotional and spiritual pain, and even despair. Many of those who have suffered in this way have also sought relief in the path of addiction. Others have experienced difficulties in significant relationships, with parents, spouses, and children. Suffering in families has been especially grave, since the damage provoked by abuse affects these vital family relationships.

Some have even had to deal with the terrible tragedy of the death of a loved one by suicide. The deaths of these so beloved children of God weigh upon the heart and my conscience and that of the whole church. To these families I express my heartfelt love and sorrow. Jesus, tortured and interrogated with passionate hatred, is taken to another place and he looks out. He looks out upon one of his own torturers, the one who denied him, and he makes him weep. Let us implore this grace together with that of making amends.

Sins of clerical sexual abuse against minors have a toxic effect on faith and hope in God. Some of you have held fast to faith, while for others the experience of betrayal and abandonment has led to a weakening of faith in God. Your presence here speaks of the miracle of hope, which prevails against the deepest darkness. Surely it is a sign of God's mercy that today we have this opportunity to encounter one another, to adore God, to look into one another's eyes and seek the grace of reconciliation.

Before God and his people I express my sorrow for the sins and grave crimes of clerical sexual abuse committed against you. And I humbly ask forgiveness.

I beg your forgiveness, too, for the sins of omission on the part of church leaders who did not respond adequately to reports of abuse made by family members, as well as by abuse victims themselves. This led to even greater suffering on the part of those who were abused and it endangered other minors who were at risk.

On the other hand, the courage that you and others have shown by speaking up, by telling the truth, was a service of love, since for us it shed light on a terrible darkness in the life of the church. There is no place in the church's ministry for those who commit these abuses, and I commit myself not to tolerate harm done to a minor by any individual, whether a cleric or not. All bishops must carry out their pastoral ministry with the utmost care in order to help foster the protection of minors, and they will be held accountable.

What Jesus says about those who cause scandal applies to all of us: the millstone and the sea (cf. Mt 18:6).

By the same token we will continue to exercise vigilance in priestly formation. I am counting on the members of the Pontifical Commission for the Protection of Minors, all minors, whatever religion they belong to; they are little flowers which God looks lovingly upon.

I ask this support so as to help me ensure that we develop better policies and procedures in the universal church for the protection of minors and for the training of church personnel in implementing those policies and procedures. We need to do everything in our power to ensure that these sins have no place in the church.

Dear brothers and sisters, because we are all members of God's family, we are called to live lives shaped by mercy. The Lord Jesus, our Savior, is the supreme example of this; though innocent, he took our sins upon himself on the cross. To be reconciled is the very essence of our shared identity as followers of Jesus Christ. By turning back to him, accompanied by our most holy Mother, who stood sorrowing at the foot of the cross, let us seek the grace of reconciliation with the entire people of God. The loving intercession of Our Lady of Tender Mercy is an unfailing source of help in the process of our healing.

You and all those who were abused by clergy are loved by God. I pray that the remnants of the darkness which touched you may be healed by the embrace of the Child Jesus and that the harm which was done to you will give way to renewed faith and joy.

I am grateful for this meeting. And please pray for me, so that the eyes of my heart will always clearly see the path of merciful love, and that God will grant me the courage to persevere on this path for the good of all children and young people. Jesus comes forth from an unjust trial, from a cruel interrogation, and he looks in the eyes of Peter, and Peter weeps. We ask that he look at us and that we allow ourselves to be looked upon and to weep and that he give us the grace to be ashamed, so that, like Peter, forty days later, we can reply: "You know that I love you"; and hear him say: "go back and feed my sheep"—and I would add—"let no wolf enter the sheepfold."

The Gospel in Your Pocket

September 1, 2014
I Cor 2:1–5; Lk 4:16–30

"Jesus is present in the word of God and he speaks to us." This is why "the word of God is different even from the loftiest human words." And we must draw near to it "with an open heart, with a humble heart, with the spirit of the Beatitudes." This is the reason that Pope Francis has again suggested that one should always carry a small, pocket-sized gospel, to read it when possible and thus "to find" Jesus. He repeated this during the Mass at St. Martha's.

Resuming the morning eucharistic celebrations open to groups of the faithful—after a period of suspension during July and August—the pontiff reflected on the word of God based on the two readings from the day's liturgy, taken from, respectively, the first letter of Paul to the Corinthians (2:1-5) and from the gospel according to Luke (4:16-30).

Pope Francis underscored that, in the first reading, St. Paul "reminds the Corinthians what his message was like, how he had proclaimed the gospel," and he explained: "I did not come proclaiming to you the testimony of God in lofty words or wisdom." Paul continues, the pope added, by saying that he did not present himself in order to convince his interlocutors "with arguments, with words, even with images." The apostle chose instead "another mode, another style," and that is a "demonstration of the Spirit and power, that"—these are Paul's words—"your faith might not rest in the wisdom of men but in the power of God."

In effect, the pontiff continued, the apostle recalled that "the word of God is something different, something which is unequaled by a human word, a wise word, a scientific word, a philosophical word." The word of God, indeed, "is something else, it comes in another way": it is "different" because "it is how God speaks."

Luke confirms this in the gospel passage which tells of Jesus in the synagogue of Nazareth, "where he grew up" and where everyone "knew him as a child." In that context, the pope explained, he "began to speak and the people listened to him," commenting: "Oh, how interesting!" Then "they bore witness: they were amazed by the words he spoke." And among them they observed: "Look at him, this one! How good, this boy whom we know, how good he has become! But where must he have studied?"

However, the pontiff pointed out, Jesus "stopped them" and said to them: "Truly, I say to you, no prophet is acceptable in his own country." Thus, to those who listened to him in the synagogue "at first" it seemed "a good thing and they accepted that manner of conversation and reception." But "when Jesus began to give the word of God they became furious and they wanted to kill him." Thus "they passed from one side to the other, because the word of God is different from the word of man, even from the loftiest word of man, the most philosophical word of man."

And so, Francis asked himself, "what is the word of God like?" The letter to the Hebrews, he affirmed, "began by saying that, since ancient times, God had spoken, and he spoke to our fathers through the prophets. But in these times, at the end of that world, he spoke through the Son." In other words, "the word of God is Jesus, Jesus himself." That is what Paul was preaching when he said: "When I came to you, brethren, I did not come proclaiming to you the testimony of God in lofty words or wisdom. For I decided to know nothing among you except Jesus Christ and Christ crucified."

This is "the word of God, the only word of God," the pope

explained. And "Jesus Christ is a reason for scandal: the cross of Christ scandalizes. That is the strength of the word of God: Jesus Christ, the Lord."

It becomes so important, the pontiff said, to ask ourselves: "How do we receive the word of God?" The response is clear: "As one receives Jesus Christ. The church tells us that Jesus is present in the scripture, in his word." This is why, he added, "I have advised you many times to always carry a small gospel with you"— moreover, "it costs little" to buy it, he added, smiling—to keep it "in your purse, in your pocket, and read a passage from the gospel during the day." Some practical advice, he said, not so much "to learn" something, but mostly "to find Jesus, because Jesus actually is in his word, in his gospel." Thus, he restated, "every time I read the gospel, I find Jesus."

And what is the right attitude to receive this word? It must be received, the bishop of Rome affirmed, "as one receives Jesus, that is, with an open heart, with a humble heart, with the spirit of the Beatitudes. Because this is how Jesus came, in humility: he came in poverty, he came anointed by the Holy Spirit." Such that "he himself began his discourse in the synagogue of Nazareth" with these words: "The Spirit of the Lord is upon me, because he has anointed me to preach the good news to the poor. He has sent me to proclaim release to the captives and recovering of sight to the blind, to set at liberty those who are oppressed, to proclaim the acceptable year of the Lord."

Thus, "he is strength, he is the word of God, because he was anointed by the Holy Spirit." In this way, Francis recommended, "we too, if we want to hear and receive the word of God, we must pray to the Holy Spirit and ask for this anointing of the heart, which is the unction of the Beatitudes." Thus, to have "a heart like the heart of the Beatitudes."

As "Jesus is present in the word of God," the pope said, and "He speaks to us in the word of God, it will do us good during the day today to ask ourselves: How do I receive the word of God?" An essential question, Pope Francis concluded, again renewing his counsel to always carry the gospel with you so as to read a passage every day.

Old Women and the Theologian

September 2, 2014
1 Cor 2:10b–16; Lk 4:31–37

It is the Holy Spirit who gives "identity" to the Christian. This is why—Pope Francis said in his homily during morning Mass at St. Martha's—"you can have five degrees in theology, but not have the Spirit of God." And "you might be a great theologian but you are not a Christian," precisely "because you do not have the Spirit of God."

Thus, he pointed out, "many times we find, among our faithful, simple old women who perhaps didn't finish elementary school, but who speak to you about things better than a theologian, because they have the Spirit of Christ." And the pope offered the example of St. Paul, who despite his effective preaching had no particular academic qualifications—he had not taken courses in "human wisdom" at the Lateran or Gregorian Pontifical Universities—but he spoke to in a way pleasing to the Spirit of God.

In the passage of the gospel according to Luke proposed for the day's liturgy (4:31-37), the word "authority" appears twice. The people "were astonished by Jesus' teaching, for his word was with authority," the pope affirmed. And then again, at the very end of the passage, the gospel tells that "they were all amazed and said to one another: 'What is this word? For with authority and power he commands . . ."' Thus, Pope Francis continued, "the people were astonished because when Jesus spoke, when he preached, he had authority which the other preachers didn't have, which the other legal experts didn't have, those who were teaching the people."

The question to ask yourself is: "But what is this authority of Jesus, this new thing which astounded the people? This gift, different from the legal experts' manner of speaking and teaching?" And the answer is definitive. "This authority," the pontiff explained, "is precisely the unique and special identity of Jesus." Indeed, "Jesus was not a common preacher; Jesus was not one who taught the law like all the others. He did so in a different way, in a new way, because he had the strength of the Holy Spirit."

Pope Francis then recalled that the day before, "in the liturgy, we read that passage in which Jesus presents himself, visits his synagogue, and he speaks of himself in the words of the prophet Isaiah: "The Spirit of the Lord is upon me, because he has anointed me" and "he has sent me to proclaim." The Holy Father explained that this, too, confirms that "the authority which Jesus has comes precisely from this special anointing of the Holy Spirit: Jesus is anointed, the first Anointed One, the true Anointed One." And "this anointing gives authority to Jesus."

"The very identity of Jesus is the Anointed Being," the pontiff restated. He is "the Son of God, anointed and sent, sent to bring salvation, to bring freedom." Thus "this is the identity of Jesus, and because of this the people said: 'This man has special authority, which the legal experts who teach us do not have.' But," the pope added, "some are scandalized by this manner of Jesus, this style of Jesus."

Here then, "the liberty, the freedom of Jesus is the very anointing of the Holy Spirit." And, Francis exhorted, we can ask ourselves what our identity as Christians is." In the first letter to the

Corinthians (2:10-16), St. Paul explains that "we impart this in words not taught by human wisdom." And in this regard the pontiff highlighted that "Paul's preaching" does not emanate from "human wisdom," because his words were "taught to him by the Holy Spirit." In fact, the pope emphasized, he "preached with the anointing of the Spirit, expressing spiritual matters of the Spirit in spiritual terms."

However, Francis noted, using the very expressions of St. Paul: "The unspiritual man does not receive the gifts of the Spirit of God, . . . and he is not able to understand them because they are spiritually discerned." Thus "if we Christians do not understand the gifts of the Spirit, we do not bear and we do not offer testimony, we do not have identity."

After all, "these gifts of the spirit" seem only "a folly," such that those who lack identity are "not able to understand them."

The pontiff recalled, referring again to the letter of St. Paul, that the "spiritual man judges all things, but is himself to be judged by no one." Indeed, the pope added, again quoting the words of the apostle, "who has known the mind of the Lord? But now we have the mind of Christ, that is, the Spirit of Christ." And "this is the Christian identity: not having the spirit of the world, that manner of thinking, that manner of judging."

Ultimately, "what gives authority, what gives identity is the Holy Spirit, the anointing of the Holy Spirit." This is why, according to the pope, "people don't love those preachers, those legal experts, because they spoke truthfully about theology, but they didn't reach the heart, they didn't give freedom, they weren't capable of doing so in a manner the people identified with, because they were not anointed by the Holy Spirit." However, the pope clarified, "the authority of Jesus—and the authority of the Christian—comes from this very capacity to understand the gifts of the Spirit, to speak the language of the Spirit; it comes from this anointing of the Holy Spirit."

Pope Francis concluded by praying to the Lord to give us "the Christian identity, that which you have: give us your Spirit; give us your way of thinking, of feeling, of speaking: that is, Lord, grant us the anointing of the Holy Spirit."

Why Boast about Sins?

September 4, 2014
1 Cor 3:18–23; Lk 5:1–11

"Of what things can a Christian boast? Two things: his sins and Christ Crucified." Only one thing really counts: the encounter with Christ which changes the life of "tepid" Christians and transforms the face of "decadent" parishes and communities. This was Pope Francis' topic at morning Mass.

The pontiff spoke mainly about the liturgy's first reading from the first letter of St. Paul to the Corinthians (3:18-23). The pope explained that "in these verses that we have read during recent liturgies," Paul "speaks of the strength of the word of God." Moreover, it can be said that Paul "does theology with the word of God." And the apostle concluded with this reflection: "Let no one deceive himself. If anyone among you thinks that he is wise in this age, let him become a fool that he may become wise. For the wisdom of this world is folly with God."

Basically, the pontiff stated, "Paul tells us that the strength of God's word, which changes the heart, which changes the world, which gives us hope, which gives us life, does not lie in human wisdom." Thus "it is not in speaking well and in saying things with human intelligence. No, that is folly." Rather, "the strength of God's word comes from another place." Of course "it also passes through a preacher's heart." And this is why Paul advises all those who preach the word of God: "Become fools." He admonished them not to search for security "in the knowledge of the world." And thus the apostle continues, "let no one boast of men."

At this point one must wonder "where Paul's security is, where his security is rooted." The pope then pointed out that Paul "had studied with the most knowledgeable teachers of his time," yet he never boasted. Rather, "he boasted of only two things, and these things that Paul boasted of are precisely the place where the word of God can come and be strong." Indeed, he said of himself: "I boast only of my sins." These were "scandalous words," the pontiff said, adding that "in another verse he says: I boast only of Christ and of this crucifix." Thus "the strength of God's word is in that encounter between my sins and the blood of Christ who saves me. And when there is no such encounter, there is no strength in the heart." And when we forget that encounter, Pope Francis said, "we become worldly, we want to speak about the matters of God with human language, and this is useless" because "it is not life giving."

Thus "the encounter between my sins and Christ" is crucial. And this, Francis noted, is what happens when, in the reading from the gospel according to Luke (5:1-11), Jesus tells Simon to "put out into the deep and let down your nets for a catch." Peter responded to him: "Master, we toiled all night and took nothing! But at your word I will let down the nets." And, the pope continued, this is how "that miraculous catch" happened.

In the face of this event, "what does Peter think?" asked the bishop of Rome. He does not react with satisfaction for the catch he hadn't hoped for, nor for what he would earn from it, the pope explained. He "only sees Christ; he sees his strength and he sees himself." Therefore he kneels at Jesus' feet saying: "Depart from me, for I am a sinful man, O Lord."

For Peter, "this encounter with Jesus Christ" becomes the encounter between his sins and the strength of the Lord who saves. In that situation, the pontiff highlighted, "the sign of salvation was the miracle of the catch; the privileged place for the encounter with Jesus Christ is one's sins."

Pope Francis continued, "if a Christian is incapable of feeling himself a sinner and saved by the blood of Christ Crucified, he is a half-way Christian; he is a tepid Christian." And "when we find decadent churches, when we find decadent parishes, decadent institutions, certainly the Christians who are there have never encountered Jesus Christ, or they have forgotten that encounter with Jesus Christ."

"The strength of the Christian life and the strength of the word of God lie precisely in that moment where I, sinner, encounter Jesus Christ," the pope explained. "And that encounter turns life inside-out; it is life changing. And it gives you the strength to proclaim salvation to others." Paul's words and Luke's gospel propose "so many questions" to believers. The pontiff indicated that one should ask oneself: "Am I capable of saying to the Lord: 'I am a sinner'?" The question is not theoretical but practical, because the examination of conscience is concerned, above all, with the capacity to recognize "concrete sin." The pope then proposed other questions to ask oneself: "Am I capable of believing that he, with his blood, has saved me from sin and has given me new life? Do I trust in Christ? Do I boast of the cross of Christ? Do I also boast of my sins, in this sense?"

In this regard, Pope Francis advised going back to the moment of the "encounter with Jesus Christ," to ascertain that it has not been forgotten, by asking oneself: "Have I encountered Jesus Christ. Have I felt his strength?" These are fundamental questions, he concluded, because "when a Christian forgets this encounter he loses his strength: he is tepid, incapable of giving to others, with strength, the word of God."

NEW WINE, NEW WINESKINS

September 5, 2014
1 COR 4:1–5; LK 5:33–39

D o not have fear of making changes according to the law of the gospel: "The church asks all of us for a few changes. She asks us to leave aside fleeting structures; they aren't necessary." Instead leave room for the "law of the Beatitudes," for "joy," and for the "freedom which leads us to the newness of the gospel." These were the words of Pope Francis at morning Mass.

The pope drew upon the reading from the gospel of Luke (5:33-39) from the day's liturgy. "These scribes, these Pharisees wanted to put Jesus in difficulty, they wanted to trap him." Reminding him that John and his disciples fasted, they ask him: "You are such friends with John and your disciples are friends who seem to be just, why don't you do the same?" To which "Jesus replies, speaking of two things: he speaks to us of a feast and he speaks to us of newness."

The pontiff explained that Jesus primarily "tells us about a feast, a wedding feast, and he says: but we are in a time of feast! There is something new here, there is a feast! Something has fallen and something is renewed, made new." And it is "curious," the pope pointed out, that Jesus "at the end uses the image of wine" such that "when this verse is read it is impossible not to connect this wedding feast to the new wine of Cana." Basically, "everything is a symbol which speaks of newness," above all when Jesus says: "no one puts new wine into old wineskins." Thus "for new wine, new wineskins." This "is the newness of the gospel." Francis then asked, "What does the gospel bring us? Joy and newness."

However, he continued, "these doctors of the law were locked up in their commandments, in their rules." So much that "St. Paul, speaking about them, tells us that before faith came—that is, Jesus—we were all held as prisoners under the law." But this law was not cruel: "held but as prisoners, waiting for faith to come." Indeed, "that faith which would be revealed in Jesus himself."

The pope affirmed that the people had the law that Moses had given. And then so many of these customs and little laws that the experts and theologians had decreed." Thus "the law held them, but as prisoners. And they were waiting for freedom, for the definitive freedom that God would give to his people through his Son."

The pope recalled that St. Paul tells us, "when the time had fully come, God sent forth his Son, born of woman, born under the law, to redeem." And "the newness of the gospel is this: it is for redemption from the law." In this regard the pontiff observed: "One of you may tell me: but Father, don't Christians have laws? Yes! Jesus said: I have not come to abolish the law but to fulfill it." And the "fullness of the law, for example, is the Beatitudes, the law of love, total love, as he, Jesus, has loved us."

Thus, the bishop of Rome continued, "when Jesus reproaches these people, these doctors of the law, he admonishes them for not having safeguarded the people with the law" but for having made them "slaves of so many little laws, of so many little things that they had to do." And to have done it "without the freedom that he brings us with the new law, the law that he had sanctioned with his blood."

This then "is the newness of the gospel, which is a feast; it is joy, it is freedom." It is "that very redemption that the whole of mankind was waiting for when they were held by the law, but as prisoners." And this is also "what Jesus meant to tell us: what do we do, Jesus, now?" The answer is: "Do what is new, newness; to new wine, new wineskins." For this reason, the pope explained, one need not "have fear of making changes according to the law of the gospel, which is a law of faith." St. Paul "makes a good distinction: sons of law and sons of faith. To new wine, new wineskins." This is why "the church asks us, all of us, for a few changes. She asks us to leave aside fleeting structures; they aren't necessary! And to get new wineskins, those of the gospel."

Pope Francis then pointed out that "it is not possible to understand the mentality, for example, of these doctors of the law, these Pharisee theologians, with the spirit of the gospel. They are different things." In fact, "the gospel's approach is a different approach, which leads to the fulfillment of the law." But "in a new way: it is the new wine in new wineskins."

To the question posed by those Pharisees and scribes, the pope observed, Jesus basically responded: "We cannot fast as you do during a feast. Days will come when the bridegroom is taken away." And saying this "he was thinking of his passion; he was thinking of the times of the passion of so many Christians, where there will be a cross."

The fact remains, however, that "the gospel is newness, the gospel is a feast. And one can fully live the gospel only in a joyous heart and in a renewed heart." In this perspective the pope asked the Lord for "the grace of this observance of the law: to observe the law—the law which Jesus brought to fulfillment—in the commandment of love, in the commandments which come through the Beatitudes: those commandments of the renewed law of the newness of the gospel." May the Lord, Pope Francis concluded, "give us the grace of not being prisoners, but may he give us the grace of joy and of the freedom which brings us the newness of the gospel."

SMALL AND HOLY

September 8, 2014
ROM 8:28–30; MT 1:1-16, 18–23

G od is "the Lord of history" and also of "patience." He "walks with us." For this reason the Christian is called not to fear great things and to pay attention also to small things. Referencing St. Thomas Aquinas, this was Pope Francis' exhortation to the faithful attending Mass at St. Martha's.

The pontiff's first observation was that "when we read in Genesis the story of creation," we risk "thinking that God was a magician," complete with a "magic wand," able to do all things. But "that is not how it was." In fact, the pope explained, "God made things—each one—and he let them go with the interior, inward laws which he gave to each one, so that they would develop, so they would reach fullness." Thus "the Lord gave autonomy to the things of the universe," but "not independence." And this way, "creation went on for centuries and centuries and centuries, until it got to how it is today." Precisely "because God is not a magician, he is Creator."

Instead for man the question differs, the bishop of Rome explained. "When on the sixth day of that narrative the creation of man comes," God "gives another kind of autonomy, a bit different, but not independence: an autonomy which is freedom." And "he tells man to go on in history: God puts man in charge of creation so that he can exercise stewardship over creation and bring it to the fullness of time." The pope explained that the "fullness of time" is "what God had at heart: the coming of his Son."

In this respect the pontiff referred to the reading from the letter of St. Paul to the Romans (8:28-30) in the day's liturgy. Making the apostle's words his own, Pope Francis said that

"God predestined us, everyone, to be conformed to the image of his Son. And this is the path of humanity, it is the path of man: God wanted us to be like his Son and for his Son to be like us."

"And this is how history continued," as is also seen in the passage of the gospel according to Matthew (1:1-16, 18-23), which lists the genealogy of Jesus: "This one was the father of this one; this one fathered this one, this one fathered this one. . . But it is history," the pope affirmed. And, he noted, "in this list there are saints and also sinners; but history goes on because God wanted men to be free." However, "the day that man misused his freedom, God drove him out of paradise." The Bible tells us that "he made him a promise and man left paradise with hope: a sinner, but with hope."

The pontiff continued, indicating that "this historical list led to problems, war, hostility, sin, but also hope. They did not make their journey alone: God walked with them. Because God created an option: he created an option for time, not for the moment." He is "the God of time, he is the God of history; he is the God who walks with his children" until the "fullness of time," that is, when his Son is made man.

Now, here, the narrative is a bit repetitive; "it contains this treasure: God walks with the just and with sinners." And if the Christian recognizes himself as a sinner, he knows that God also walks with him, "with all, to reach man's final encounter with him." After all, "the gospel, which constructs this history for centuries, ends in a tiny thing, in a small village, with this story of Joseph and Mary: she was found to be with child of the Holy Spirit." Therefore "the God of the great history is also in the little story, there, because he wants to walk with each one." The pope recalled "such a beautiful phrase about this" in the Summa Theologica of St. Thomas, who says "not to fear great things, but also to acknowledge the small ones;

this is divine." Because God "is in the great things, but also in the small ones, in our small things." Moreover, he added, "the Lord who walks with God is also the Lord of patience": the patience "which he had with all these generations, with all these people who lived their history of grace and sin." God, the pope affirmed, "is patient. God walks with us, because he wants all of us to come to be conformed to the image of his Son." And "from that moment in creation in which he gave us freedom—not independence—until today, he continues to journey."

Francis then turned his thoughts to Mary, on the day of the feast of her Nativity. "Today we are in the antechamber of this story: the birth of Our Lady." And let us thus ask the Lord "in prayer to grant us unity to walk together, and peace in the heart. It is today's grace: it is how we arrive here, because our God is patient, he loves us, he accompanies us.

Thus today, the pontiff continued, "we can look to Our Lady, small, holy, without sin, pure, chosen to become the mother of God, and also to look at this history behind her, so long, for centuries." Then he asked several fundamental questions: "How do I journey in my story? Do I let God walk with me? Do I let him walk with me or do I want to walk alone? Do I let him caress me, help me, forgive me, lead me forward to reach the encounter with Jesus Christ?" Because precisely this, the Holy Father emphasized, "will be the end of our journey: to encounter the Lord."

Thus, the pope continued, there is one question which "will do us good today" to answer: "Do I let God have patience with me?" Only "by looking at this great history and also at this small village," he asserted in conclusion, "can we praise the Lord and humbly ask that he grant us peace, that peace of heart which he alone can give us, which he gives us only when we let him walk with us."

On Jesus' List

September 9, 2014
1 Cor 6:1-11; Lk 6:12-19

The Lord is the "one who prays, who chooses, and who is not ashamed to be close to the people." Commenting on a passage from the gospel according to Luke (6:12-19), Pope Francis highlighted these three characteristics which "effectively portray Jesus' personality" and which also motivate our "trust in him: we trust him because he prays, because he has chosen us, and because he is close."

The pontiff first spoke about prayer. Luke says that the Lord "went out into the hills to pray; and all night he continued in prayer to God." He "was praying for us. It seems a bit strange that he has come to grant us salvation, he has that power," and yet, Pope Francis observed, "he so often prays, he even talks about it," recalling the phrase addressed to Peter during the Last Supper: "I have prayed for you."

Jesus has prayed and continues to pray for us: "he is the intercessor," the bishop of Rome declared. "Even now, as he stands before the Father in heaven, this is his work: to intercede. He is the great intercessor." It is not by chance that "when we pray to the Father, at the beginning of Mass, every day, at the end of the prayer we say to the Father: 'We ask this of you through Jesus Christ, our Lord, who prays for us.'" Because in that very moment the Son is before the Father "praying for us."

This truth "should give us courage." Because in "times of difficulty or of need," Pope Francis urged, one must remember: "You are praying for me. Jesus is praying for me. Jesus prays to the Father for me." Thus, the pope added, this "is his work today: to pray for us, for his church." And even if "we often forget that Jesus is praying for us," this is indeed "our strength." The strength of being able "to say to the Father: 'But if you, Father, do not see us, look at your Son who is praying for us.' From the first moment Jesus prays: he prayed when he was on earth and he continues to pray now for each of us, for all the church."

Passing to the second moment in the gospel scene—"And when it was day, he called his disciples, and chose from them twelve, whom he named apostles"—the pontiff pointed out that "it was he who chose; and he clearly says so: 'You did not choose me but I chose you.'" Therefore, this approach of Jesus also gives us courage, because we have that assurance: "I am chosen, I am chosen by the Lord. On the day of baptism he chose me." St. Paul was conscious of this, and thinking of this he said: "He chose me, from the very womb of my mother."

And why are we "chosen" as Christians? Francis finds the answer to this question in the love of God, who "does not look to see whether one's face is ugly or fair: He loves! And Jesus does the same: he loves and chooses with love. And he chooses everyone." On his "list" there are no important people "according to worldly criteria: there are common people." The only feature which characterizes them all is that "they are sinners." Jesus chose sinners. He chooses sinners. And this is the accusation that the doctors of the law, the scribes, make: "This one eats with sinners, he speaks with prostitutes."

But this is how Jesus is and thus "he calls everyone," the bishop of Rome continued, recalling the parable of the marriage feast of the son: "When the guests did not come, what did the master do? He sent his servants: 'Go and bring everyone home! The good and the bad,' the gospel says. Jesus chose everyone. He chose sinners and for this he is reproached by the doctors of the law." His criterion is love, which is clear from "the day of our baptism," when "we were officially chosen." And in that choice "is the love of Jesus." Indeed, he "looked at me and he said to me: you!" It is enough to ponder the choice of "Judas Iscariot, who became the traitor, the greatest sinner for him. But he was chosen by Jesus."

Finally the third moment, described in the day's gospel with these words: "And he came down with them and stood on a level place, with a great crowd of his disciples and a great multitude of people from all Judea and Jerusalem and the seacoast of Tyre and Sidon, who came to hear him and to be healed of their diseases . . . And all the crowd sought to touch him." The scene essentially presents a "Jesus close to the people. He is not a professor, a teacher, a mystic who distances himself and speaks from a pulpit," but rather a person who "is in the midst of the people; he lets himself be touched; he lets the people call him. This is how Jesus is: close to the people."

And this closeness, Pope Francis explained, "is not a new thing for him: he emphasized it in his manner of conduct; however, it is something which comes from God's first choice for his people. God tells his people: 'Consider, which people have a God as close as I am to you?'" God's closeness to his people, the pontiff concluded, "is Jesus' closeness to the people." All the crowd sought to touch him, because a power emanated from him which healed everyone. Close in this way, in the midst of the people."

Foolish Christians

September 11, 2014
1 Cor 8:1b–7, 11-13; Lk 6:27–38

Being Christian means being "a bit foolish," at least according to worldly logic. And this is by no means self-reflexive, since one cannot manage to do anything alone, and it is actually not to frighten us but to rescue us that the grace of God comes. During morning Mass, Pope Francis proposed these basic features of Christian life which are centered on the newness of the gospel and which overturn worldly criteria.

Advising that chapter six of the gospel according to St. Luke—the day's liturgy focused on verses 27–38 in particular—be read and reread, even four times if necessary, the pontiff recalled that Jesus gave us "the law of love: to love God and to love one another as brothers." And, the pope added, the Lord did not fail to explain it "a bit further, with the Beatitudes" which nicely summarize "the Christian approach."

In the day's gospel passage, however, Jesus goes a step further, explaining in greater detail "to those who surround him to hear him." Let us look, said Pope Francis, first of all at the "verbs Jesus uses: love; do good; bless; pray; offer; do not refuse; give." The pope continued that, with these words, "Jesus shows us the path that we must take, a path of generosity." He asks us first and foremost to "love." And we ask, "who must I love?" He answers us, "your enemies." And, with surprise, we ask for confirmation: "our actual enemies?" "Yes," the Lord tells us, actually "your enemies!"

But the Lord also asks us to "do good." And if we do not ask him, "to whom?" he tells us straightaway, "to those who hate us." And this time too, we ask the Lord for confirmation: "But must I do good to those who hate me?" And the Lord's reply is again, "yes."

Then he even asks us to "bless those who curse us." And to "pray" not only "for my mom, for my dad, my children, my family," but "for those who abuse us." And "not to refuse anyone who begs from you." The "newness of the gospel," the pope explained, lies in the "giving of oneself, giving the heart, to those who actually dislike us, who harm us, to our enemies." The passage from Luke reads: "And as you wish that men would do to you, do so to them. If you love those who love you, what credit is that to you?" It would merely be an "exchange: you love me, I love you." But Jesus reminds us that "even sinners"—and by sinners he means pagans—"love those who love them." This is why, Francis pointed out, "there is no credit."

The passage continues: "And if you do good to those who do good to you, what credit is that to you? For even sinners do the same." Again, the pope said, it is simply "an exchange: I do good to you, you do good to me!" And yet the gospel adds: "And if you lend to those from whom you hope to receive, what credit is that to you?" The pontiff's clear-cut response: no credit, because "it's a bargain." St. Luke then indicates, "even sinners lend to sinners, to receive as much again."

All of Jesus' reasoning, Pope Francis affirmed, leads to a firm conclusion: "Love your enemies instead. Do good, and lend, expecting nothing in return. Without interest. And your reward will be great." And thus "you will be sons of the Most High."

It is therefore evident, the pope continued, that "the gospel is a new message that is difficult to carry forward." In a word, it means "go behind Jesus." Follow him. Imitate him. Jesus does not answer his Father by saying, "I shall go and say a few words, I shall make a nice speech, I shall point the way and then come back." No, Jesus' response to the Father is, "I shall do your will." And indeed, on the Mount of Olives he says to the Father: "Thy will be done." And thus "he gives his life, not for his friends" but "for his enemies!"

The Christian way is not easy, the pope recognized, but "this is it." Therefore, to those who say, "I don't feel like doing this," the response is "if you don't feel like it, that's your problem, but this is the Christian way. This is the path that Jesus teaches us," the pontiff said. This is the reason to "take the path of Jesus, which is mercy: be merciful as your Father is merciful." Because "only with a merciful heart can we do all that the Lord advises us, until the end." And thus it is obvious that "the Christian life is not a self-reflexive life" but "it comes outside of itself to give to others: it is a gift, it is love, and love does not turn back on itself, it is not selfish: it gives itself!"

The passage of St. Luke concludes with the invitation not to judge and to be merciful. However, the pontiff said, "it often seems that we have been appointed judges of others: gossiping, criticizing, we judge everyone." But Jesus tells us: "Judge not and you will not be judged; condemn not, and you will not be condemned; forgive, and you will be forgiven." And so, "we say it every day in the Our Father: forgive us as we forgive." In fact "if I do not first forgive, how can I ask the Father to forgive me?"

There is also, the pope said, another really beautiful image in the gospel reading: "Give and it will be given to you." And here "Jesus' heart can be seen to grow, and he makes this promise which is perhaps an image of heaven." The Christian life, as Jesus presents it, seems truly to be "folly," Francis indicated. St. Paul himself speaks of "the folly of the cross of Christ, which is not part of the wisdom of the world." For this reason, "to be a Christian is to become a bit foolish, in a certain sense." And "to renounce that worldly shrewdness in order to do all that Jesus tells us to do. And, if we make an accounting, if we balance things out, it seems to weigh against us." But "the path of Jesus" is "magnanimity, generosity, the giving of oneself without measure." He "came into the world" to save and he gave himself, "he forgave, he spoke ill of no one, he did not judge."

Of course, the pontiff recognized, "being Christian isn't easy" and we cannot "become Christian" with our own strength; we need "the grace of God." Therefore, there is a prayer, said the pope, which should be said every day: "Lord, grant me the grace to become a good Christian, because I cannot do it" alone.

Francis concluded the meditation by acknowledging that "a first reading" of chapter six of Luke's gospel "is unnerving." But, he suggested, "if we take the gospel and we give it a second, a third, a fourth reading," we can then ask "the Lord for the grace to understand what it is to be Christian." And "also for the grace that he make Christians of us. Because we cannot do it alone."

MENDING HOLES IN THE FABRIC OF THE CHURCH

September 12, 2014
1 COR 9:16–19, 22B, 27; LK 6:39–42

Christians risk "disqualification," as St. Paul admonishes, if they insist on performing brotherly correction without charity, truth, and humility, making room for hypocrisy and gossip. In truth this service to others requires one, first of all, to recognize oneself as a sinner and not to sit in judgment, as the pope recalled during Mass at St. Martha's Guest House.

Francis pointed out straightaway that "in recent days the liturgy has led us to meditate on many Christian attitudes: to give, to be generous, to serve others, to forgive, to be merciful." These "are approaches," he explained, "which help the church to grow." But today especially, "the Lord makes us consider one of these approaches, which he has already spoken of, and that is brotherly correction." The bottom line is: "When a brother, a sister from the community makes a mistake, how does one correct them?"

Always through the liturgy, the pope continued, "the Lord has given us advice on how to correct" others. But "today he resumes and says: one must correct him or her, but as a person who sees and not as one who is blind." Pope Francis referred to the gospel according to Luke (6:39-42): "Can a blind man lead a blind man?"

Thus to offer correction it is necessary to see clearly. And to follow several rules of behavior that the Lord himself proposed. "First of all, the advice he gives to correct a brother—we heard the other day," the pope recalled. "It is to take aside your brother who made the error and speak to him, telling him, 'brother, in this regard, I believe you did not do right!'"

And "to take him aside," indeed, means "to correct him with charity." It isn't possible to correct someone without love and charity. That would be like "performing surgery without anesthesia," resulting in a patient's painful death. And "charity is like anesthesia which helps him to receive the care and to accept the correction." Here then is the first step toward a brother: "take him aside, gently, lovingly, and speak to him."

The pope then, turning also to the many religious present at the celebration at St. Martha's, advised that one always speak "with charity," without wounding, "in our communities, parishes, institutions, religious communities, when one must say something to a sister, to a brother."

Along with charity, it is necessary to "tell the truth" and never "say something that isn't true." In fact, Pope Francis pointed out, "many times in our communities things are said to another person that aren't true: they are libelous." Or, "if they are true" they "harm the reputation of that person."

In this respect, according to the pope, the following may be a way to approach a brother: "I am telling you this, to you, what you have done. It is true. It isn't a rumor that I heard." Because "rumors wound, they are insults to a person's reputation, they are strikes at a person's heart." And so "the truth" is always needed, even if at times "it isn't good to hear it." In every case if the truth "is told with charity and with love, it is easier to accept." This is why it is necessary to speak "the truth with charity: this is how one must speak to others about faults."

Jesus speaks of the third rule, humility, in the passage of Luke's gospel: correct others "without hypocrisy, that is, with humility." It is good, the bishop of Rome advised, to point out to oneself "if you must correct a tiny flaw there, consider that you have so many" that are greater. The Lord says this effectively: first take the log out of your own eye, and then you will see clearly to take out the speck from the eye of another. Only in this way "will you not be blind" and "will you see clearly" to truly help your brother. Thus "humility" is important in order to recognize that "I am a greater sinner than him, a greater sinner than her." Afterwards "I must help him and her to correct this" flaw.

"If I do not perform brotherly correction with charity, do not perform it in truth, and do not perform it with humility, I become blind," the pope admonished. And if I do not see, it is asked, how do I "heal another blind person?"

In substance, "fraternal correction is an act to heal the body of the church." Francis described it with a compelling image: it is like mending "a hole in the fabric of the church." However, one must proceed "with much sensitivity, like mothers and grandmothers when they mend," and this is the very manner with which "one must perform brotherly correction."

On the other hand, Francis indicated, "if you are not capable of performing fraternal reproof with love, with charity, in truth, and with humility, you will offend, damage that person's heart; you will create gossip that wounds and you will become a blind hypocrite, as Jesus says." Indeed, the day's reading from the gospel of Luke reads: "You hypocrite, first take the log out of your eye." And while it is necessary to recognize oneself as being "a greater sinner than the other," as brothers, however, we are called to "help to correct him."

The pontiff did not fail to offer practical advice. There is, he said, "a sign which perhaps can help us: when one sees something wrong and feels that he should correct it" but perceives "a certain pleasure in doing so," then it is time to "pay attention, because that is not the Lord's way." Indeed, "in the Lord there is always the cross, the difficulty of doing something good." And love and gentleness always come from the Lord.

This whole line of reasoning on fraternal correction, the pope continued, demands that we not judge. Even if "we Christians are tempted to act as scholars," almost as if to "move outside the game of sin and of grace, as if we were angels."

This is a temptation that St. Paul also speaks of in his first letter to the Corinthians (9:16-19, 22-27): "lest after preaching to others I myself should be disqualified." The apostle therefore reminds us, "a Christian who, in community, doesn't do things, even brotherly correction, in charity, in truth, and with humility, is disqualified." Because "he has not managed to become a mature Christian."

Francis concluded by praying that the Lord "help us in this brotherly service, so beautiful and so agonizing, of helping brothers and sisters to be better," pushing ourselves "to always do so with charity, in truth and with humility.

THREE WOMEN

September 15, 2014
1 Cor 11:17–26, 33; Jn 19:25—27

Two women and mothers—Mary and the church—bring Christ to a third woman, who resembles the first two but is "little": our soul. The pope reaffirmed, with these wholly female images, that without the motherhood of Mary and the church we would not have Christ. "We are not orphans," he recalled during the Mass celebrated in the chapel at St. Martha's Guest House.

Francis highlighted right away that "the church, in the liturgy, leads us twice, for two days, one after the other, to Calvary": in fact, "yesterday she made us contemplate the cross of Jesus, and today his mother at the cross" (Jn 19:25-27). In particular, "yesterday she had us speak a word: glorious." A word which refers to the "cross of the Lord, because it brings life, it brings us glory." But "today the strongest word of the liturgy is: mother." The cross is glorious; the mother humble, gentle," the mother whom the liturgy celebrates today as Our Lady of Sorrows.

Meditating on the Mother leads us directly to Jesus as Son. Referring to the day's reading (Heb 5:7-9), the pontiff pointed out that "in the passage from the letter to the Hebrews, Paul emphasizes three strong words, speaking of Jesus the Son: he learned, he obeyed, and he suffered." Jesus, in essence "learned obedience and suffered." Thus, "it is the opposite of what had befallen our father Adam, who had not learned what the Lord commanded, who had neither suffered nor obeyed." Moreover, the pope stated, "this passage from the letter to the Hebrews reminds us of another passage from the letter to the Philippians: although he was in the form of God, he did not consider it an inalienable right; he renounced it, he humbled himself, and took the form of a servant. This," Pope Francis continued, "is the glory of the cross of Jesus" who "came to the world to learn to be a man and, being man, to walk with men. He came to the world in obedience and he obeyed." But "this obedience was learned through suffering."

"Adam left paradise with a promise," he proceeded, "which went on throughout many centuries. Today, with this obedience, with this self-denial, this humbling of Jesus, that promise has become hope." And "the people of God journey with confident hope."

Mary too, "the Mother, the New Eve, as Paul himself called

her, follows this path of her son: she learned, she suffered, and she obeyed." She "became 'Mother.' We could say that she is the 'anointed Mother,'" the pontiff affirmed, and the same is true for the church.

Thus, this is "our hope: we are not orphans, we have mothers": first of all Mary. And then the church, who is Mother "when she follows the same path of Jesus and Mary: the path of obedience, the path of suffering, and when her approach is to constantly learn the way of the Lord."

"These two women—Mary and the church—carry on the hope which is Christ; they give us Christ, they generate Christ in us," the bishop of Rome emphasized. Thus "without Mary, Jesus Christ would not have been; without the church, we cannot go forward." They are "two women and two mothers."

"Mary," Francis explained, "remained steadfast at the cross. She was bonded with the son because she had accepted him and she knew, more or less, that a sword awaited her. Simon had told her so." Mary is "the steadfast Mother," he continued, "who gives us certainty on this path of learning, of suffering, and of obedience." And mother church is also "steadfast when she adores Jesus Christ and she guides us, teaches us, shelters us, helps us on this path of obedience, of suffering, of learning this wisdom of God."

Moreover, the pontiff again affirmed, "our soul also takes part in this, when it opens itself to Mary and to the church: according to monk and abbot Isaac of Stella, our soul is also female and likewise resembles Mary and the church." Thus "today, looking at the cross, this woman—steadfastly following her son, suffering in order to learn obedience—we see the church and we see our mother." But "we also see our little soul, which will never be lost if it too continues to be a woman close to those two great women who accompany us in life: Mary and the church."

Francis concluded by recalling that "as our fathers left paradise with a promise, today we are able to go forward with hope: the hope we are given by Mary, steadfast at the cross, and our hierarchical holy mother church."

When God Visits

September 16, 2014
1 Cor 12:12–14, 27–31a; Lk 7:11–17

With his witness, a Christian must show others the same attitudes with which God visits his people: closeness, compassion, the capacity to restore hope. Pope Francis affirmed this during Mass at St. Martha's.

"God has visited his people" is an expression which is "repeated in the scripture," the pontiff noted. He immediately referred to the narrative in the gospel of Luke, which tells of the resurrection of the widow's son in Nain (7:11-17). They are words, he stated, which have "special meaning," different from that of such expressions as "God has spoken to his people," or "God has given the commandments to his people," or even "God has sent a prophet to his people."

In the statement "God has visited his people," the pope said, "there is something extra, something new." This phrase can be found in the scripture; it is written, for example, "God visited [Naomi] in her old age and made her a grandmother." And likewise, the pontiff added, scripture "tells of Elizabeth, Mary's cousin: God visited her and made her a mother."

So "when God visits his people, it means that he is present in a special way." And, Francis highlighted, recalling the event in Nain, "in this gospel passage, where it describes the resurrection of the young man, the son of the widowed mother, the people speak these words: 'God has visited us.'"

Why use this exact expression? Is it only because Jesus "performed a miracle?" the pontiff asked. In reality, there is "more." In fact the key issue is to understand "how God visits."

The bishop of Rome indicated that God visits "first of all with his presence, with his closeness." In the passage from the day's liturgy "it is written that Jesus went to a city called Nain, and his disciples and a great crowd went with him." In essence, "he was close to the people: a close God who is able to understand the heart of the people, the heart of his people." Then, Luke recounts, "he sees that procession and he draws near." Thus "God visits his people," he is "in the midst of his people he draws near." Hence, "closeness is God's way."

Additionally, the pope observed, "there is an expression repeated many times in the Bible: "The Lord was moved by great compassion." And it is that "same compassion which, the gospel says, he had when he saw so many people like sheep without a shepherd." So it is a fact that "when God visits his people he is close to them, he draws near and feels compassion; he is moved." He is "deeply moved, as he was in front of Lazarus' tomb." He is moved like the father in the parable, when he sees the prodigal son return home.

"Closeness and compassion: this is how the Lord visits his people," Francis remarked. And "when we want to proclaim the gospel, to spread the word of Jesus, this is the way." However, "the other way is that of the teachers, the preachers of that time: the doctors of the law, the scribes, the Pharisees." Characters "far removed from the people," who "spoke well, taught the law well." But they were also "distant." And their way "was not a visit from the Lord; it was something else." Such that "the people did not feel this as a grace, because it lacked closeness; it lacked compassion and suffering with the people."

Adding to "closeness" and "compassion," the pope proposed "another word which is characteristic of the Lord's visit to his people." Luke writes: "And the dead man sat up, and began to speak. And he gave him to his mother." Thus "when God visits his people, he restores hope to the people. Always!"

In this regard, Francis pointed out that "one can preach the word of God brilliantly," and "there have been many great preachers: but if these preachers do not manage to sow hope, their preaching is useless. It is in vain."

This very image proposed by the gospel of Luke, the pope said, can bring a full understanding to "what is meant by God's visit to his people." We understand "by seeing Jesus in the midst of that great crowd; by seeing Jesus draw close to that funeral procession and the crying mother, and he tells her 'Do not weep,' and perhaps he caresses her; by seeing Jesus give the mother back her son, alive." In this way, the pontiff concluded, we can "ask for the grace that our Christian witness may be the bearer of God's visit to his people, that is, of closeness which sows hope."

THE SCENT OF A SINNER

September 18, 2014
1 COR 15:1–11; LK 7:36–50

The Lord saves "only when we open the heart" in the "truth of our sins." This was the lesson that Pope Francis drew from the day's reading from the gospel according to Luke (7:36–50). The passage relates the story of the sinful woman who, at lunch in a Pharisee's home, without being invited, approaches Christ with "a flask of ointment" and "standing behind him at his feet, weeping," she begins to "wet his feet with her tears," then wiping them "with the hair of her head," kisses them and anoints them with ointment.

The pontiff explained that the very "recognition of sins, our misery, the recognition of what we are and what we are capable of doing or have done is the door that opens to the caress of Jesus, to the forgiveness of Jesus, to the word of Jesus: Go in peace; your faith has saved you, because you have been brave, you have been courageous in opening your heart to him who alone can save you." In this regard the pope repeated an expression especially dear to him: "the privileged place for the encounter with Christ is our sins."

Pope Francis commented that to the untrained ear this "would almost seem heresy, but even St. Paul said it" in the second letter to the Corinthians (12:9), when he affirmed boasting of "only two things: of his sins and of the risen Christ who saved him."

The bishop of Rome introduced his reflection by reconstructing the scene described in the gospel passage. He explained that the man "who invited Jesus to lunch was a person of a certain level, cultured, perhaps an academic. He wanted to hear Jesus' teaching because, as a good and cultured person, he was unsettled," and sought to "know more." And "it doesn't seem that he was a bad person," and nor were "the others who were at the table." Until a female figure bursts into the banquet: deep down "an ill-mannered woman" who "actually enters where she was not invited. One who was not cultured or, if she was, she did not show it here." In fact "she enters and does what she wants to do: without apologizing, without asking permission." The pope observed, "Jesus lets her do" all this.

It is here that reality is revealed behind the facade of good manners, with the Pharisee who begins to think to himself: "If this man were a prophet, he would know who and what sort of woman this is who is touching him, for she is a sinner." This was not a "bad" man, yet "he was unable to understand the woman's gesture. He was unable to understand the basic gestures of the people." Perhaps, Francis emphasized, "this man had forgotten how to caress a child, how to console a grandmother. In his theories, in his thoughts, in his government life—because perhaps he was a councilor to the Pharisees—he had forgotten the first gestures of life that we all, right at birth, began to receive from our parents." In other words he "was far from reality." Only in this way, the pope continued, can his "accusation" toward Jesus be explained: "This is a holy man! He speaks to us of beautiful things, he performs some magic; he is a healer; but in the end he does not know the people, because if he knew what sort of woman this is he would have said something."

Here then are two very different "approaches": on one side is that of the "man who sees and qualifies," he judges; and on the other, that of the "woman who cries and does seemingly mad things," because she uses ointment which "is expensive, it's costly." The pontiff paused on the particular fact that in the gospel the word "anoint" is used to signify that the "woman's ointment anoints: it has the capacity to become an unction," to the contrary of the Pharisee's words, which "do not touch the heart, do not touch the body, do not touch reality."

Between these two very antithetical figures is Jesus, with "his patience, his love," his "will to save everyone," which "lead him to explain to the Pharisee the meaning of what this woman is doing" and to reproach him, although "with humility and tenderness," for having lacked "courtesy" toward him. "I entered your house; you gave me no water for my feet, but she has wet my feet with her tears and wiped them with her hair. You gave me no kiss, but from the time I came in she has not ceased to kiss my feet. You did not anoint my head with oil, but she has anointed my feet with ointment."

The pope also highlighted that the gospel does not say "how the story ends for this man," but it clearly tells "how it ends for the woman: 'your sins are forgiven!'" This sentence scandalized "those who were at the table with him, who began to say among themselves, 'Who is this, who even forgives sins?'," while Jesus continues straight on his path and "says that phrase so often repeated in the gospel: 'Go in peace, your faith has saved you!'" In other words, "she is told that her sins are forgiven" while "Jesus only shows and explains gestures to the others, that is, what they haven't done for him." It is a difference which Francis wanted to stress: in the woman's behavior "there is so very much love," while regarding that of the dinner companions, Jesus does not say that love is lacking, "but he makes it understood." As a result, "the words of salvation—'Your faith has saved you!'—he says only to the woman, who is a sinner. And he tells her because she has managed to weep for her sins, so to speak. 'I am a sinner.'" On the contrary, "he doesn't say it to those people" who, although they were not "bad," actually "believed they weren't sinners." To them "the sinners were the others: the publicans, the prostitutes."

Here then is the lesson of the gospel: "Salvation enters the heart only when we open the heart in the truth of our sins." Of course, the bishop of Rome reasoned, "none of us will go to make the gesture that this woman did," because it is "a cultural gesture of that period; but we all have the opportunity to weep, we all have the opportunity to open ourselves and say: Lord save me! We all have the opportunity to encounter the Lord." This is also because, the pope indicated, "to the other people in this gospel passage, Jesus says nothing. But in another passage he will say those terrible words: "Hypocrites, because you are detached from reality, from the truth!" And yet, in reference to the example of this sinful woman, he will caution: "Think hard! It will be the prostitutes and the publicans to go before you into the kingdom of heaven." Because they, the pontiff concluded, "feel they are sinners" and "they open their heart in the confession of sins, at the encounter with Jesus, who gave his blood for all of us."

FEAR OF RESURRECTION

September 19, 2014
1 COR 15:12-20; LK 8:1-3

Christian identity is fulfilled for us only with the resurrection, which will be "like a reawakening." This is why Pope Francis advised "being with the Lord," walking with him as disciples, in order that the resurrection may begin here and now. But "without fear of the transformation that our body will undergo at the end of our Christian journey."

The pontiff focused precisely on the essence of the resurrection in his homily during Mass. Drawing from the day's reading from the first letter of St. Paul to the Corinthians (15:12-20), the pope first explained that the apostle "has to make a correction which is difficult for that time: that of the resurrection." Indeed, "the Christians believed that yes, Christ is risen, he went away, he finished his mission, he helps us from heaven, he accompanies us," but what was "not very clear" for them was "the following result that we too will be raised."

In reality, Francis affirmed, "they thought in another way: yes, the dead are justified, they will not go to hell—very good!—but they will go a bit in the cosmos, in the air, there, the soul before God: only the soul." But "they did not understand; the resurrection did not enter their mind": that is, that "we too will be raised."

"There was strong resistance," the pope pointed out, and it was so "from the first days." Thus, Peter himself, who "had contemplated Jesus in his glory on Mount Tabor, on the morning of the resurrection, rushed to the grave," believing that the Lord's body had been stolen. He did this because "a true resurrection had not entered their mind." Their "theological" vision, the pontiff explained, ended with triumph. Such that "on the day of the ascension they said: But tell me, Lord, now will you free the kingdom of Israel?"

They did not understand "our passage from death to life through the resurrection," the bishop of Rome explained. "Not even Mary Magdalene, who loved the Lord so much," understood. And she too thought: "They stole the body!"

The disciples did not understand "the resurrection either of Jesus or of Christians." In the end they only accepted "that of Jesus, because they saw it"; but the resurrection "of Christians was not understood in the same way." They were convinced that "we will go to heaven, but nothing unusual" such as: "the dead will be raised."

The same thing happens "when Paul goes to Athens and begins to speak" about the resurrection: "the wise men and philosophers from Greece are frightened" the pope recalled. The question is that if "the resurrection of Christ is a miracle, perhaps a frightening thing, the resurrection of Christians is a scandal: they cannot understand it!" And this is why "Paul reasons this very clearly: If Christ is raised, how can some of you say that there is no resurrection of the dead? If Christ is raised, the dead will also be raised."

The pontiff observed that there is "resistance to the transformation, resistance that the work of the Spirit, which we received in baptism, transforms until the end, at the resurrection." And "when we speak about this, our language says: but I want to go to heaven, I do not want to go to hell!" However, "we stop there." And "none of us says: I will be revived like Christ!"

For us as well, Francis continued, "it is difficult to understand this." Very difficult. It is easier to imagine a sort of "cosmic pantheism" and to think: "We will be in the contemplation, there, in the world, the world will be changed." Thus, there is "resistance to being changed, which is the word which Paul uses: 'We will be changed. Our body will be changed.'" This resistance is "human," the pope recognized. Such that "when a man or a woman must undergo surgery" they are very frightened because either something will be removed or something else will be placed inside them; they "will be transformed, so to speak." And so there is fear. But, the pope clarified, "with the resurrection, we will all be transformed."

"This is the future that awaits us," the pope emphasized, "and this leads us to put up great resistance to the transformation of our body," but "resistance also to the Christian identity." And, he added: "Perhaps we do not have much fear of the apocalypse of the Evil One, of the Antichrist who must come first; perhaps we do not have much fear. Perhaps we do not have much fear of the call of the archangel or of the sound of the trumpet: but, the victory will be the Lord's." Yet we have "fear of our resurrection: all of us will be transformed." And "that transformation will be the end of our Christian journey."

"This temptation to not believe in the resurrection of the dead," the pope explained, "was born in the early church, in the first days of the church. Paul, in about the year 50, must clarify this very thing to the Thessalonians and speak about it once or twice." And "at the end, to console them, to encourage them, he says one of the most hope-filled phrases in the New Testament: 'At the end we will be with him.'" And it will be "to stay with the Lord, this way, with our body and with our soul." This is our "Christian identity: to stay with the Lord." It is an affirmation which, the pontiff remarked, is certainly not "news." Indeed, "it is the first thing said by the first disciples." In fact, "when John the Baptist signals Jesus as the Lamb of God and the two disciples come with him, the gospel reads: 'and they stayed with him that day.'"

"We will be raised to stay with the Lord," the pontiff affirmed, "and the resurrection begins here, as disciples, if we stay with the Lord, if we walk with the Lord. This is the path toward the resurrection. And if we are accustomed to staying with the Lord, this fear of the transformation of our body falls away."

In reality the resurrection "will be like a reawakening," Francis clarified, repeating the words of Psalm 17[16]: "when I awake, I shall be satisfied with beholding thy form." And "Job also tells us: whom 'my eyes shall behold.' Not spiritually: with my body, with my eyes, transformed." This is why one must not "have fear of the Christian identity," which "does not end with a temporal triumph, it does not end with a good mission." Because "the Christian identity is fulfilled with the resurrection of our bodies, with our resurrection: the end is there, that we are sated with the image of the Lord."

For this reason, the pope indicated, "the Christian identity is a journey; it is a path where one stays with the Lord, like those two disciples who stayed with the Lord all that evening." Thus "even our whole life is called to be with the Lord to remain, to stay with the Lord, after the call of the archangel, after the sound of the trumpet." And the pope recalled in conclusion that St. Paul, in the letter to the Thessalonians, "ends with this line of reasoning with this phrase: 'Comfort one another with these words.'"

Two Conditions

September 23, 2014
Prov 21:1-6, 10-13; Lk 8:19-21

The word of God is not "a comic strip" to be read, but a lesson to be listened to with the heart and to be practiced every day—a commitment accessible to all, because although "we have made it a bit difficult," Christian life is "simple, simple." In fact, "to listen to the word of God and practice it" are the only two "conditions" established by Jesus for those who want to follow him.

For Pope Francis, this sums up the meaning of the readings

from Mass on Tuesday, September 23. During the Mass at St. Martha's, the pontiff paused on the passage from the gospel according to Luke (8:19-21) which speaks of Jesus' mother and brethren who "could not reach him because of the crowd." Beginning with the observation that Jesus spent most of his time "on the street, with the people," the bishop of Rome pointed out that among the many who followed him there were people who heard "in him a new authority, a new way of speaking"; they heard "the power of salvation" that he offered. In this regard, the pope indicated that "it was the Holy Spirit who touched their hearts."

However, the pope noted that there were also people mixed among the crowd who followed Jesus with ulterior motives. Some "out of convenience," others perhaps out of a "desire to be better." A bit like us today, he said, in that "so often we go to Jesus because we need something and then we forget him there, alone." The story repeats itself, seeing that even then Jesus sometimes admonished those who followed him. That is what happens, for example, when Jesus says to the people: "You come to me not to hear the word of God but because I fed you the other day"; or with the ten lepers, of whom only one came back to thank him, while "the other nine were happy with their health and forgot about Jesus."

Despite all this, the pope affirmed, "Jesus continued to speak to the people" and to love them to the point of defining "that immense crowd as 'my mother and my brethren.'" Thus, the family of Jesus are "those who listen to the word of God" and "put it into practice." This, Pope Francis stated, "is the Christian life: nothing more. Simple, simple. Perhaps we have made it a bit difficult, with so many explanations that no one understands, but Christian life is like this: listening to the word of God and practicing it. This is what we prayed for in the psalm: 'Guide me, Lord, in the way of your commands,' of your word, of your commandments, in order to practice" them.

He then invited us to "truly listen to the word, in the Bible, in the gospel," meditating on the scriptures to put their content into practice every day. But, the pontiff clarified, if we scan the gospel superficially, "this is not listening to the word of God: this is reading the word of God, as if one would read a comic strip." While to listen to God's word is "to read it" and ask oneself, "What does this say to my heart?" Only in this way, in fact, "does our life change." This happens "every time we open the gospel and read a passage and ask ourselves: 'Is God speaking to me with this, is he saying something to me?'"

This means "to listen to the word of God, to listen with the ears and listen with the heart, to open the heart to God's word." On the other hand, "Jesus' enemies listened to Jesus' words but they were close by in order to try to find a mistake, to make him slip up" and make him lose "authority. But they never asked themselves: 'What is God telling me with these words?'"

Moreover, the pontiff added, "God does not speak only to all but he speaks to each one of us. The gospel was written for each one of us. And when I pick up the Bible, when I pick up the gospel and read it, I must ask myself what the Lord is saying to me." This, then, "is what Jesus says that true relatives do, his true brethren: they 'listen to the word of God with the heart.' And then, he says, 'they put it into practice.'"

Of course, Francis recognized, "it is easier to live calmly without being concerned with the requirements of God's word." However, "the Father also did this work for us." Indeed, the commandments are really "a means of practicing the word of the Lord." And the same holds true for the Beatitudes. The pope observed that there in that passage from the gospel according to Matthew "is everything we must do in order to put the word of God into practice."

Last "are the works of mercy," which also appear in the gospel of Matthew, in chapter 25. In short, these are examples "of what Jesus wants when he asks us to put the word 'into practice.'"

In conclusion, the pontiff summarized his reflections, recalling that "so many people followed Jesus," some of them "for the novelty," others "in need of hearing a good message," but in reality there were not many who then effectively "practiced the word of God." Yet "the Lord did his work because he is merciful and he forgives everyone; he calls everyone back, he awaits everyone, because he is patient."

Even today, the pope highlighted, "so many people go to church to hear the word of God, but perhaps they do not understand the preacher when he preaches something a bit difficult; or they do not want to understand. Because this is also true: many times, our heart does not want to understand." But Jesus continues to welcome us, "even those who go and listen to the word of God and then betray him," as did Judas who calls him "friend." The Lord, Francis reiterated, "always plants his word," and in exchange "he asks only for an open heart to listen to it and good will to put it into practice. This is why today's prayer is that of the psalm: 'Guide me, Lord, in the way of your commands,' that is, on the path of your word, so that, with your guidance, I may learn to practice it."

TRUE IDENTITY

September 26, 2014
ECCLES 3:1-11; LK 9:18-45

The identity card of a Christian should be the same in all respects as that of Jesus. And the cross is what we have in common and what saves us. Because "if each one of us is not willing to die with Jesus, to be raised with him, we do not yet have a true Christian identity." Pope Francis outlined this basic profile of every believer during Mass at St. Martha's.

The pope's reflection arose from the question "But who do you say that I am?" that Jesus posed to his disciples in the day's reading from the gospel according to Luke (9:18-22). Francis pointed out immediately that Jesus "protected his true identity in a special manner." He let the people say of him: "He is a great one, no one speaks like he does; he is a great teacher, he heals us!" However, "when someone would come close to his true identity, he would stop them." It is important to understand the reason for this approach.

The bishop of Rome recalled that "from the very beginning, with the temptation in the wilderness, the devil tried to get Jesus to confess his true identity," telling him: "If you are the righteous one, if you are the Son of God, do this! Show me that you are!" And then, "after several healings or in a few encounters, the demons who were chased away shouted at him" with these very words: "You are the righteous one! You are the Son of God!" But, the pope noted, "he silenced them."

"The devil," Pope Francis commented, "is intelligent; he knows more theology than all the theologians together." And so he wanted Jesus to confess: "I am the Messiah! I have come to save you!" This confession, he explained, would have caused "great confusion in the people," who would have thought: "This one comes to save us. Now let's form an army, let's get rid of the Romans: this one will give us freedom, happiness!"

And precisely so "the people would not err, Jesus safeguarded the crux of his identity." The gospel of Luke recounts how the Lord "puts his disciples to the test." He does so after returning from a solitary place where he had gathered his thoughts in prayer. He went before them and asked: "Who do the people say that I am?" The disciples answered: "John the Baptist; but others say, Elijah; and others, that one of the old prophets has risen." This answer, Francis pointed out, "refers to what we heard yesterday in the gospel passage: Herod was perplexed because he didn't know whether this Jesus was John the Baptist or another." Thus, the disciples said the same thing in response. And here, the Lord poses the question directly to them: "But who do you say that I am?" Peter answered for all of them: "The Christ of God. This is your identity! You are the Messiah! You are the Christ of God! You are the anointed one, the one we have been waiting for!" But even in this situation Jesus "charged and commanded them to tell this to no one."

He thus wanted to "protect his identity." Then, Jesus "explains; he begins to give a catechesis on his true identity." And he says that "the Son of Man must suffer many things, and be rejected by the elders and chief priests and scribes, and be killed and on the third day be raised." This, he tells the disciples, is the very path "of your freedom, this is the path of the Messiah, of the righteous one: the passion, the cross." But they, the pontiff indicated, "do not want to understand, and in the passage from Matthew it is seen that Peter rejects this: "No, no, Lord!" And so, with the disciples, "Jesus begins to open the mystery of his identity," confiding in them: "Yes, I am the Son of God. But this is my journey: I must take this path of suffering."

The pope indicated that Jesus allows the crowd to speak of his identity only on Palm Sunday. He does so "only there, because it is the beginning of the final march." And "Jesus does this in order to prepare the disciples' hearts, the hearts of the people to understand this mystery of God: God's love is so great, sin is so bad that he saves us this way, with this identity in the cross."

After all, Francis continued, "one cannot understand Jesus Christ the Redeemer without the cross." And, "we can go so far as to think that he is a great prophet, he does good things, he is a saint. But Christ the Redeemer cannot be understood without the cross." However, he explained, "the hearts of the disciples, the hearts of the people were not prepared to understand this: they had not understood the prophecies, they had not understood that he was truly the sacrificial lamb." Only on Palm Sunday did he allow the people to cry out: "Blessed is he who comes in the name of the Lord!" And "if this people does not shout," Pope Francis said, "the stones would cry out!"

"The first confession of his identity," the pontiff affirmed, "was made at the end, after his death." It was already made "before his death, indirectly," by "the good thief"; but "after his death the first confession was made: 'Truly this was the righteous one! The *dikaios*!'" And these words, the pope highlighted, were spoken by "a pagan, the centurion."

Francis observed that "the pedagogy of Jesus, even with us, is like this: step by step he prepares us to understand him well." And "he also prepares us to accompany him with our crosses on the path toward redemption." In essence, "he prepares us to be Cyrenes in order to help him carry the cross." Such that "without this, our Christian life is not Christian." It is only "a spiritual, good life"; and Jesus himself becomes only "the great prophet." Reality is different: Jesus has saved us all by making us take "the same path" that he chose. Thus, "our identity as Christians must also be protected." And one must not fall into the temptation of "believing that to be a Christian is a merit; it is a spiritual journey of perfection: it is not a merit, it is pure grace." It is also "a journey of perfection," but "alone it does not suffice." Because, the pontiff concluded, "to be a Christian is to be a part of Jesus in his own identity, in that mystery of the death and resurrection."

ANGELS AND DEMONS

September 29, 2014
DAN 7:9-10, 13-14; JN 1:47-51

The fight against the subtle plans of destruction and dehumanization brought forth by the devil—who "presents things as if they were good," even inventing "humanistic explanations"—is "an everyday reality." And unless we fight "we will be defeated." But we have the certainty of not being alone in this fight, because the Lord entrusted to the archangels the task of defending man. Pope Francis recalled the actual role of Michael, Gabriel, and Raphael during morning Mass at St. Martha's.

The pontiff began by pointing out that "the two readings we heard—both that from the prophet Daniel (7:9-10, 13-14) and that from the gospel according to John (1:47-51)—speak to us about glory: the glory of heaven, the court of heaven, the adoration in heaven." Thus, he explained, "there is glory" and "in the midst of this glory there is Jesus Christ." In fact, Daniel says: "I saw in the night visions, and behold, with the clouds of heaven there came one like a son of man, and he came to the Ancient of Days and was presented before him. And to him was given dominion and glory and kingdom, that all peoples, nations, and languages should serve him." Here, Francis said, is "Jesus Christ, before the Father, in the glory of heaven."

The day's liturgy also reintroduces this reality in the gospel. Thus, the pope continued, "to Nathaniel, who was astonished, Jesus says: 'you shall see greater things than these. . . you will see heaven opened, and the angels of God ascending and descending upon the Son of Man.'" And the Holy Father used "the image of Jacob's ladder: Jesus is at the center of the glory, Jesus is the glory of the Father." A glory which, the bishop of Rome clarified, "is promised in Daniel, is promised in Jesus. But it is also a promise made in eternity."

The pontiff then referred to the "other reading" from Revelation (12:7-12). In this text as well, he indicated, "glory is spoken of, but as a battle." In fact, it reads: "Now war arose in heaven: Michael and his angels fighting against the dragon; and the dragon and his angels fought, but they were defeated and there was no longer any place for them in heaven. And the great dragon was thrown down, that ancient serpent, who is called the Devil and Satan, the deceiver of the whole world—he was thrown down to the earth, and his angels were thrown down with him." It is the "battle between the Devil and God," the Holy Father explained. But "this battle happens after Satan seeks to destroy the woman who is about to give birth to her son." Because, the pope stated, "Satan always seeks to destroy man: that man whom Daniel saw there, in glory, and who Jesus told Nathaniel would come in glory." The pope said further that, "from the beginning, the Bible tells us about this: Satan's seduction to destroy. Perhaps out of envy." And in this regard, in reference to Psalm 8, Francis highlighted that the angel so highly intelligent "could not bear this humiliation on his shoulders, that an inferior creature could be made superior; and he sought to destroy him."

"The task of the people of God," the pontiff explained, "is to guard the man himself: the man Jesus. Guard him, because he is the man who gives life to all men, to all humanity." And, from their side, "the angels fight in order that man wins." Thus, "the man, the Son of God, Jesus and man, humanity, all of us, fight against all these things that Satan does to destroy him."

Indeed, Francis affirmed, "so many projects, except for one's own sins, but so many, many projects for the dehumanization of man are his works, simply because he hates man." Satan "is subtle; the first page of Genesis says so. He is subtle, he presents things as if they were good. But his intention is destruction."

In the face of Satan's work "the angels defend us: they defend man and they defend God-man, the superior man, Jesus Christ, who is the perfection of humanity, the most perfect one." This is why "the church honors the angels, because it is they who will be in the glory of God—they are in the glory of God—because they defend the great hidden mystery of God, that is, that the Word came in the flesh." He is exactly "who they [Satan and his cohorts] want to destroy; and when they cannot destroy Jesus the person, they seek to destroy his people; and when they cannot destroy the people of God, they make up humanistic explanations that actually go against man, against humanity and against God."

This is why, the pope said, "the battle is a daily reality in Christian life, in our family, in our people, in our churches." Such that "unless we fight, we will be defeated." However, "the Lord has mainly given this task to the angels," that is, "to fight and win."

And also for this reason, he added, "the final song of the Apocalypse, after this fight, is so beautiful: 'Now salvation is fulfilled, the strength and the Kingdom of our God and the power of his Christ, because our brothers' accuser has fallen, the one who accused them day and night before our God.'" The objective, therefore, was destruction and, as a result, there is this "victory song" in the Apocalypse.

Recalling the feast of the archangels Michael, Gabriel, and Raphael, the pope affirmed that this was an especially suitable day to turn to them. And also "to recite that old but beautiful prayer to Michael the archangel, that he continue to fight to defend humanity's greatest mystery: that the Word became man, died, and rose again." Because "this is our treasure." And, Francis concluded, let us ask that the archangel Michael continue "to fight to guard it."

PRAYERS IN THE DARKNESS

September 30, 2014
JOB 3:1-3, 11-17, 20-23; LK 9:51-56

During Mass at St. Martha's Pope Francis called for prayer, like that of the church, for those everywhere who suffer as Jesus did, even in today's world. He invoked prayer for, above all, "those of our brothers and sisters who, in order to be Christians, are driven from their homes and are left with nothing," for the elderly who are left aside and the sick alone in hospitals: for all those who are living through "dark times."

The pontiff's reflection arose from the day's first reading from the book of Job (3:1-3, 11-17, 20-23), which contains "a prayer" that the pope deemed "a bit special; the Bible itself says that it is a curse," he explained. In fact, "Job opened his mouth and cursed" the day he was born. He complained "about what happened to him" in these words: "Let the day perish wherein I was born . . . Why did I not die at birth, come forth from the womb and expire? . . . For then I should have lain down and been quiet . . . Or why was I not as a hidden untimely birth, as infants that never see the light?"

The bishop of Rome pointed out in this regard that "Job, a rich man, a righteous man who truly adored God and followed the path of the commandments," said these things after he "lost everything." He was put to the test: he lost his whole family, all his possessions, his health, and his whole body had become afflicted. In other words, "in that moment he lost his patience and he said these things. They were bad! But he was used to speaking the truth and this was the truth that he felt in that moment." To the point of saying, "I am alone. I am abandoned. Why? Let the day perish wherein I was born, and the night which said, 'A man-child is conceived.'"

In Job's words, the pope recognized a sort of "curse against his whole life," highlighting that it is declared during the "dark moments" of his life. And the same thing also happens in Jeremiah, in chapter 20: "Cursed be the day on which I was born!" Words which beg the question, "Is this man blaspheming?" This man, all alone, with these words, "is he blaspheming? Does Jeremiah blaspheme? Jesus, when he laments—'Father, why have you abandoned me?'—is he blaspheming? This is the mystery."

The pontiff confided that many times in his pastoral experience, he himself hears "people who are living in difficult, sorrowful situations, who have lost so much or who feel alone and abandoned and come to complain and to ask these questions: Why? They rebel against God." And the pope's answer is: "Continue to pray in this way, because this too is a prayer." As was that of Jesus, when he asked the Father: "Why have you abandoned me?" and like that of Job. Because "to pray is to become truthful before God. One prays with reality. True prayer comes from the heart, from the moment that one is living." It is "prayer in moments of darkness, in the moments of life where there is no hope" and when "the horizon cannot be seen"; to the point that "many times our memory is lost and we have nowhere to anchor our hope."

Hence the relevance of God's word, because today too, "many people are in Job's situation. So many good people, like Job, do not understand what has happened to them. So many brothers and sisters who have no hope." The Pontiff's thought immediately went "to the great tragedies" such as those of Christians being driven from their homes and deprived of everything, who wonder, "But Lord, I believed in you. Why?" Why "is it a curse to believe in you?" It is the same for "the elderly left aside," for the sick, for people alone in hospitals. It is, in fact, "for all these people, these brothers and sisters of ours, and for us too, when we walk the path in the dark," that "the church prays." And in doing so, "she takes this sorrow upon herself."

An example in this sense comes from another of the day's readings, Psalm 87, which reads: "For my soul is full of troubles, and my life draws near to Sheol. I am reckoned among those who go down to the Pit; I am a man who has not strength, like one forsaken among the dead, like the slain that lie in the grave, like those whom thou dost remember no more." In exactly this way, Francis stated, "the church prays for all those who are in the trial of darkness."

In addition to these people, those "without illness, without hunger, without important needs" also have "a bit of darkness in the soul." There are situations in which "we believe we are martyrs and we stop praying," saying we are angry with God, to the point of no longer even going to Mass.

On the contrary, the passage from the day's scripture "teaches us the wisdom of prayer in the darkness, of prayer without hope." And the pope cited the example of St. Teresa of the Child Jesus, who, "in her last year of life, tried to think of heaven" and "felt within her a voice that said, 'Do not be foolish, do not make believe. Do you know what is waiting for you? Nothing!'"

Many times all of us, after all, "experience this situation. And many people think of ending up in nothingness." But St. Teresa protected herself from this pitfall: she "prayed and asked for the strength to go on, in the dark. This is called 'entering with patience.'" It is a virtue that is cultivated with prayer, because, the bishop of Rome admonished, "our life is too easy, our complaints are complaints for the theatre" when compared to the "complaints of so many people, of many brothers and sisters who are in the dark, who have almost lost their memory, almost lost hope, who are outcasts, even from themselves."

The Holy Father recalled that Jesus himself had journeyed on "this path: from the evening on the Mount of Olives to the last words on the cross: 'Father, why have you abandoned me?'" The pope offered two concluding thoughts "that may be useful." The first was a call to "prepare yourself, for when darkness comes." Darkness "will come, perhaps not as it did to Job," perhaps not as difficult, "but we will have a time of darkness." Everyone will. This is why it is necessary to "prepare the heart for that moment." This second closing thought was a call "to pray, as the church prays, with the church, for so many brothers and sisters who suffer being outcast from themselves, in darkness and in suffering, with no hope at hand."

We All Have an Angel

October 2, 2014
Ex 23:20-23a; Mt 18:1-5, 10

W e all have an angel who is always beside us, who never abandons us and helps us not to lose our way. And if we know how to be like children we can avoid the temptation of being self-sufficient, which leads to arrogance and even to extreme careerism. During the Mass celebrated at St. Martha's, Pope Francis recalled the definitive role of guardian angels in a Christian's life.

Francis pointed out two images—the angel and the child—which "the church shows us in today's liturgy." The book of Exodus (23:20-23a), in particular, proposes "the image of the angel" that "the Lord gives to his people to help them on their journey." It reads, in fact: "Behold, I send an angel before you, to guard you on the way and to bring you to the place which I have prepared."

Thus, the pope commented, "life is a journey, our life is a journey that leads us to the place that the Lord has prepared." But, he stated, "no one walks alone: no one!" Because "no one can walk alone." And, "should one of us believe he is able to walk alone, he would be greatly mistaken" and "would fall into that mistake, so harmful, which is arrogance: believing that one's self is great." He would also end up having that attitude of "sufficiency" that leads one to say: "I can, I can do it" myself.

Instead, the Lord gives a clear indication to his people: "Go, you will do what I tell you. You will journey in your life, but I will give you help which will continuously remind you what you must do." And thus "he tells his people what the attitude with the angel should be." The first recommendation is: "Give heed to him." And then, "hearken to his voice, do not rebel against him." Therefore, in addition to "respect" one must also be able to "listen" and "not rebel."

At the basis, the pope explained, "is that docile but non-specific attitude of obedience owed to the Father, which is precisely filial obedience." It is in essence "that obedience of wisdom, that obedience of listening to advice and making a better choice based on advice." And, he added, it is necessary "to have an open heart to seek and heed advice."

The gospel passage from Matthew (18:1-5, 10) offers the second image, that of the child. "The disciples," the bishop of Rome commented, "argued about who was the greatest among them. There was an internal dispute: careerism. These men, who were the first bishops, were tempted by careerism" and said among themselves: "I want to become greater than you." In this regard, Francis remarked: "It is not a good example that the first bishops did this, but it is the truth."

From his side "Jesus teaches them the true attitude": calling a child to him, he puts the child in their midst, the pope said, referring to Matthew. And in doing so he reveals "the docility, the need for advice, the need for help, because a child is the very symbol of the need for help, of docility in order to go forward."

"This is the way," the pontiff indicated, and not that of determining "who is the greatest." In truth, he stated, repeating the words of Jesus: whoever humbles himself like a child will be "the greatest." And here the Lord "makes that mysterious connection that cannot be explained, but it is true." He says, in fact: "See that you do not despise one of these little ones; for I tell you that in heaven their angels always behold the face of my Father who is in heaven."

In essence, Francis suggested, "it is as if he said: if you have this attitude of docility, this attitude of listening to advice, of an open heart, of not wanting to be the greatest, that attitude of not wanting to walk the path of life alone, you will be closer to the attitude of a child and closer to the contemplation of the Father."

"According to church tradition," the pope continued, "we all have an angel with us, who guards us, who makes us hear things." After all, he said, "we have often heard: 'I should do this this way . . . this is not good; be careful!'" It is really "the voice of our travel companion." We can be "certain that he will lead us to the end of our life with his advice." This is why it is necessary to "hearken to his voice; do not rebel against him." On the other hand, "rebellion, the desire to be independent, is something that we all have: it is arrogance itself, which our father Adam had in the earthly paradise." At this point the pope instructed each one: "Do not rebel, follow his advice!"

In truth, the pope confirmed, "no one walks alone, and none of us can think he is alone: this companion is always there." Of course, it happens that "when we don't want to listen to his advice, to hear his voice, we tell him: 'Go away!'" But "it's dangerous to drive away our travel companion, because no man, no woman can advise him/herself: I can give advice to another, but I cannot advise myself." Indeed, Francis recalled, "it is the Holy Spirit who advises me, it is the angel who advises me," and this is something "we need."

The pope urged that this "doctrine on the angels" not be considered "a bit fanciful." It is rather one of "truth." It is "what Jesus, what God said: 'I send an angel before you, to guard you, to accompany you on the way, so you will not make a mistake.'"

Francis concluded with a series of questions so that each one can examine his/her own conscience: "How is my relationship with my guardian angel? Do I listen to him? Do I bid him good day in the morning? Do I tell him: 'guard me while I sleep?' Do I speak with him? Do I ask his advice? Is he beside me?" We can answer these questions today, Pope Francis said. Each one of us can do so in order to evaluate "the relationship with this angel that the Lord has sent to guard me and to accompany me on the path, and who always beholds the face of the Father who is in heaven."

SALVATION OUR WAY

October 3, 2014
JOB 38:1, 12-21, 40:3-5; LK 10:13-16

Man experiences within himself "the tragedy of not accepting God's salvation" because he would prefer "to be saved in his own way." Jesus even reaches the point of tears over man's "resistance," and repeatedly offers his mercy and his forgiveness. However, we cannot say "Save us, Lord, but" do it "our way!" Pope Francis noted during Mass at St. Martha's.

In the gospel passage from Luke (10:13-16), Jesus "appears to be a little angry," and "he speaks to these people to reason with them," saying: "If marvels had happened among you in the pagan cities, you would have already, for some time, been wearing sack cloth and ashes, you would have converted. But you, no." Thus, Jesus traces "the outline of the whole history of salvation: it is the tragedy of not wanting to be saved; it is the tragedy of not accepting the salvation of God." It is as if we were to say: "Save us, Lord, but" do it "our way!"

Jesus himself recalls many times that "these people rejected the prophets; they stoned those who had been sent to them because they were a bit troublesome." The idea is always the same: "We want salvation, but we want it our way! Not how the Lord wants it."

We are facing the "tragedy of resisting being saved," the pontiff said. It is "a legacy that we have all received," because "in our heart too, there is this seed of resistance to being saved the way the Lord wants to save us."

In the context of the passage of the gospel according to Luke, Jesus is seen "speaking to his disciples who have returned from mission." And he says to them too: "'He who hears you hears me, and he who rejects you rejects me, and he who rejects me rejects him who sent me.' Your fathers did the same with the prophets." Again the idea of wanting "to be saved" our way. Certainly "the Lord saves us with our freedom," the pope indicated, adding, however, that "we want to be saved, not with freedom but with our own autonomy": we want to "make the rules."

This, Francis noted, is "precisely the tragedy of the stories of salvation, from the first moment." It is first of all "a tragedy of the people," because "the people rebel many times, in the desert, for example." However, he added, "with trials, the people mature: they become more mature." And thus, "they recognize in Jesus a great prophet and they also say: 'God has visited his people.'"

On the other hand, he continued, "it is actually the ruling class that closes the doors to the way that God wants to save us." In this sense "the powerful dialogues between Jesus and the ruling class of his time are understandable: they argue, they put him to the test, they lay traps to see if he falls," because they have "resistance to being saved."

In confronting this attitude Jesus says to them: "I don't understand you! You are like those children: we played the flute for you and you didn't dance; we sang a sad song for you and you didn't weep. What do you want?" The answer is again: "We want salvation to be done our way." It comes back to this "closure" to God's modus operandi.

Then, "when the Lord goes forward," the pope recalled,

"doubts also begin in the group close to them." John mentions this in chapter 6 of his gospel, giving voice to all those who say of Jesus: "This man is a bit strange, how can he give us his flesh to eat? But perhaps it is a little strange." Someone probably said these things and, Francis affirmed, even "his disciples began to turn back." Thus "Jesus looked at the Twelve" and he told them: "If you too want to go . . ."

There is no doubt, the pontiff explained, that "this word is harsh: the word of the cross is always harsh." But it is also "the only door to salvation." And "the faithful accept it: they sought Jesus to be healed" and "to hear his word." Indeed, they said: "This man speaks with authority, not like our class, the Pharisees, the doctors of the law, the Sadducees, who spoke in terms that no one understood." For them salvation was in fulfilling the countless commandments "that their intellectual and theological fever had created." However, "the poor people could not find an exit to salvation." They found it, though, in Jesus.

In the end, however, "they did the same as their fathers: they decided to kill Jesus," the pope stated. The Lord finds fault with this manner of behavior: "Your fathers killed the prophets, but to clear your conscience, you build them a fine monument." Thus, "they decide to kill Jesus, that is, to get rid of him, because, they say, "this man will cause us problems: we don't want this salvation! We want a well-organized, reliable salvation. We don't want this one!" As a result, "they also decide to kill Lazarus, because he is the witness to what Jesus brings: life," as Lazarus is "raised from the dead."

"With this decision, that ruling class nullifies God's power," the bishop of Rome said, recalling that "today in the prayer at the beginning of Mass, we splendidly praised the omnipotence of God: Lord, let your almighty power be revealed, above all in mercy and forgiveness." The "tragedy of resistance to salvation" leads one not to believe "in mercy and in forgiveness" but in sacrifice. And it compels one to want "everything well organized, everything definite."

It is "a tragedy," Francis recalled, which "even each one of us has inside." For this reason he offered several questions for examining the conscience: "How do I want to be saved? My way? According to a spirituality that is good, that is good for me, but that is set, having everything defined and no risks? Or in a divine manner, that is, on the path of Jesus, who always surprises us, who always opens the doors for us to that mystery of the almighty power of God, which is mercy and forgiveness?"

The pontiff assured that when Jesus "sees this tragedy of resistance, and also when he sees ours, he weeps." He "wept in front of Lazarus' tomb; he cried looking at Jerusalem" as he said, "You who kill the prophets and stone all those who are sent to you, how often would I have gathered your children together as a hen gathers her brood under her wings!" And he also weeps "facing this tragedy of not accepting his salvation as the Father wants it."

Pope Francis therefore urged us to "consider that this tragedy is in our heart," asking that each of us ask ourselves: "What do I think the path of my salvation is like: that of Jesus or another? Am I free to accept salvation or do I confuse freedom with autonomy, wanting my salvation, the one that I believe is fair? Do I believe that Jesus is the master who teaches us salvation or do I go everywhere to hire a guru who teaches me about another one?" Do I take "a more reliable path or do I seek refuge under the roof of rules and of many man-made commandments? And do I feel confident this way, and with—this is a bit hard to say—this confidence, do I buy my salvation, which Jesus bestows gratuitously, with the gratuitousness of God?" All these questions, which "will do us good to ask ourselves today," culminated in the pope's concluding proposal: "Am I resistant to the salvation of Jesus?"

Lest We Forget

October 7, 2014
Gal 1:13-24; Lk 10:38-42

What is prayer? It means "remembering our history, before God. Because our history" is "the history of his love for us." During the Mass at St. Martha's, Pope Francis chose "remembering" as the guiding principle of his homily.

To introduce his reflection, the Holy Father first explained that the Bible recalls so many times "that the Lord chose his people and accompanied them during the walk in the desert, throughout life." In essence, "He was close to them," having chosen them and having promised "to lead them to a land of joy, of happiness"; he walked with this people and forged a covenant with them.

Moreover, just as "God did with his people," the pontiff added, bringing the discussion up to date, "he has done and does with each one of us." Indeed, Francis continued, "we have been chosen." And it is "a grace" so obvious that it would suffice to ask: "Why am I a Christian and not that one there, far away, who has never even heard Jesus spoken of?" It is "a loving grace," Francis highlighted, recalling that the Lord "walks with us, on the path of life." He is "beside us," having promised us "joy and having made a covenant with us."

Then came an invitation to "remember this reality" in daily prayer, not with abstract but specific recollection as St. Paul does in the day's first reading (Gal 1:13-24). St. Paul says, brethren, "you have heard of my former life in Judaism, how I persecuted the church of God violently and tried to destroy it."

The pope noted, in this regard, that the apostle "begins his presentation" not by saying, "I'm good, I'm this one's son, I have a certain nobility . . . " On the contrary, he shows himself for what he is: "I was a persecutor, I was bad." And in this way, "Paul remembers his journey, and thus he begins to remember from the beginning," as his words testify, God, "who had set me apart before I was born, and had called me through his grace . . ." The same is true for us, the bishop of Rome clarified, who "are Christians," for "each of us, because he has chosen us and the choice is his. It's not ours. It is by grace; it is a gift."

The call to "remember" arises from the realization that this approach is "not a very common tendency among us. We forget things, we live in the moment, and then we forget the history." However, the pope pointed out, "each of us has a history: a history of grace, a history of sin, a history of the journey." This is why "it's good to pray with our history." Exactly like "Paul, who recounts a piece of his history," saying: "He chose me. He called me. He saved me. He has been my companion along the way." To the point that even the people who knew about his life also repeated the same words: "He who once persecuted us now goes and proclaims the faith which he at one time wanted to destroy."

Therefore, "remembering one's own life is giving glory to God." And also, "remembering our sins, from which the Lord saved us, is giving glory to God." After all, even Paul "says that he boasts of only two things: of his own sins and of the grace of God Crucified, of his grace." In other words, the apostle "remembered his sins," boasting of having been a sinner, because Christ Crucified saved him. "This," the pope emphasized, "was Paul's recollection." And "this is what Jesus himself asks us to remember." It is enough to consider what the Lord says to Martha: "You are anxious and troubled about many things" but only "one thing is needful," while "Mary has chosen the good portion." Which? "Hearing the Lord and remembering." This is because "one cannot pray every day as if we had no history. Each of us has his or her own. And with this history at heart" we pray. In this case our model is Mary; yet we are more similar to Martha, because like her "many times we are distracted by work, by the day, by doing those things we have to do," and we wind up forgetting our history.

The history of "our relationship with God," Pope Francis recalled, is a history that "doesn't begin on the day of baptism: it is sealed there." In reality, it begins "when God, throughout eternity, watched us and chose us." In other words it is a history which "begins in the heart of God." And thus, to pray means "to remember the choice that God made about us; to remember our covenant journey." This means asking oneself whether "this covenant has been respected" or not. And because fundamentally "we are sinners," to pray means first of all "to remember the promise that God" makes to us and that "he never betrays" this promise "that is our hope."

Leading up to his conclusion, Pope Francis emphasized that "this is the true prayer," recommending that our prayer begin with the beautiful Psalm 139[138], which was proclaimed during the day's Liturgy of the Word: "O Lord, thou hast searched me and known me! Thou knowest when I sit down and when I rise up; thou discernest my thoughts from afar. Thou searchest out my path and my lying down, and art acquainted with all my ways . . . For thou didst form my inward parts, thou didst knit me together in my mother's womb. I praise thee, for thou art fearful and wonderful. Wonderful are thy works!" Because, he said, "this is to pray."

He Always Gives More

October 9, 2014
Gal 2:2, 7-14; Lk 11:1-4

"Ask, and it will be given you; seek, and you will find; knock, and it will be opened to you. For every one who asks receives, and he who seeks finds, and to him who knocks it will be opened" (Lk 11:9-10). At the morning Mass at St. Martha's, Pope Francis returned to meditate on the theme of prayer. He paused on the day's reading from the gospel of Luke, which speaks of the man who asks, and on the love of God who answers and gives in overabundance.

After recalling the text of the collect prayer recited before the Liturgy of the Word—"O God, source of all good, hear the prayers of your people beyond every wish and all merit, pour out your mercy upon us: forgive our conscious fears and bestow that which prayer does not dare to hope"—the pontiff began his reflection pointing out that "God's mercy is not only forgiving— we all know this—but being generous and giving more and more . . . " Pausing on the invocation "and bestow that which prayer does not dare to hope," Francis highlighted: "Perhaps in prayer we ask for this and that, and he always gives us more! Always, always more."

The pope then resumed the thread of the gospel narrative, recalling that, a few verses before the passage offered in the day's liturgy, the apostles asked Jesus to teach them to pray as John had done with his disciples. "And the Lord taught them the Our Father." Afterwards the gospel goes on to speak of the "generosity of God," of that "mercy of which he always gives more, more than what we believe can be given."

Pope Francis went to the heart of the text: "'Which of you who has a friend will go to him at midnight . . . ' There are three words, three key words in this passage: friend, Father, and gift." This is the idea linked to the everyday experience of each person. In our life, the pontiff said, there are golden friends "who would give their life for a friend," and there are other more or less good ones, but a few are friends in a more profound way. There are not very many of these: "The Bible tells us 'one, two or three . . . no more.' Then the others are friends, but not like these."

Along the lines of the passage from Luke, the pope continued:

"I go to his house and ask, I ask, and in the end he feels bothered by the intrusion; he gets up and gives what the friend asks." The very "bond of friendship" sees that "we are given what we ask." But, he explained, "Jesus takes a step forward and speaks of the Father," posing these questions to his listeners: "What father among you, if his son asks for a fish, will instead of a fish give him a serpent; or if he asks for an egg, will give him a scorpion?" From here the following reassurance: "If you, then, who are evil, know how to give good gifts to your children, how much more will the heavenly Father give . . . !" This means "not only the friend who accompanies us on the journey of life helps us and gives us what we ask; but also the heavenly Father, this Father who loves us so much," to the point that he concerns himself—Jesus says—with feeding the birds of the field."

In this way, Pope Francis indicated, the Lord "wants to reawaken trust in prayer." Then, turning again to the gospel of Luke, he quoted: "Ask, and it will be given you; seek, and you will find; knock, and it will be opened to you. For every one who asks receives, and he who seeks finds, and to him who knocks it will be opened" (11:9-10). The pontiff explained: "This is the prayer: ask, seek the way, and knock at the heart of God, the friend who accompanies us, the Father" who loves all of his creatures.

At the end of the passage, the pope pointed out a phrase which "seems a little cryptic: 'If you, then, who are evil, know how to give good gifts to your children,' will your heavenly Father give much more than you ask? Yes! He 'will give the Holy Spirit to those who ask him!'" This is precisely "the gift, this is the 'more' of God." Because the Father, the pontiff underlined, "never gives you a gift, something you ask him for, like this, without wrapping it well, without something more that makes it more beautiful." And "what the Lord, the Father, gives us that is 'more' is the Spirit: the true gift of the Father is what prayer does not dare to hope." Man knocks at God's door with prayer to ask for grace.

And "he, the Father, gives me that and more: the gift, the Holy Spirit."

It is this, the pope emphasized, the dynamic of prayer, which "one does with a friend, who is the companion on the journey of life, one does with the Father and one does in the Holy Spirit." The true friend is Jesus: it is he, in fact, "who accompanies us and teaches us to pray. And our prayer must thus be Trinitarian." It is a very important point of emphasis for Pope Francis who, approaching his conclusion, recalled a classic dialogue he has had many times with the faithful: "Do you believe? Yes, yes! What do you believe in? In God! But what is God for you? God, God!" A rather generic, abstract concept, which, for the bishop of Rome, does not fit reality. Because, he stated, "the Father, the Son, and the Spirit exist: they are persons, not an idea in the air." In other words, he specified, "this 'mist God' does not exist: people exist!"

The pontiff's final message in brief: "Jesus is the companion on the journey who gives us what we ask; the Father who cares for us and loves us; and the Holy Spirit who is the gift, is that 'more' that the Father gives, for which our conscience does not dare to hope."

The Heart on Guard

October 10, 2014
Gal 3:7-14; Lk 11:15-26

Do we guard our heart well? Do we protect it from the demon's constant attempts to enter it and dwell there? These were among the questions asked by Pope Francis during Mass at St. Martha's Guest House, reflecting on the day's reading from the gospel of Luke (11:15-26). It presents "a sad story," he said, which begins with Jesus, who casts out a demon, "and ends with the moment when the demons return to the heart of the person from whom they had been cast out."

It is a recurring situation in the life of every man because, the pontiff recalled, quoting the passage from Luke: "When the unclean spirit has gone out of a man, he passes through waterless places seeking rest; and finding none he says, 'I will return to my house from which I came.'" Here, then, is where the demon, finding the heart at peace, "goes and brings seven other spirits more evil than himself, and they enter and dwell there." And thus, "the latter state of that man becomes worse than the former."

The demon in fact, the bishop of Rome explained, never gets discouraged. "He has patience" and he repeatedly returns, even "at the end of life," because he "doesn't give up what he wants for himself."

Jesus, too, felt this reality: in the gospel of Luke we read that "after the temptation in the wilderness" the demon left him alone for a while, but then "kept coming back." And the demons "set traps for him" up until the end, until his passion, "up to the cross," telling him, "If you are the Son of God. . . come, come to us; this way we can believe." And, Francis explained, what also happens to us when someone tempts us, asking us: "Are you capable?" And they challenge us maliciously, saying: "No, you aren't capable." This is why "Jesus speaks of a strong man, fully armed, the guard of his own palace, who guards his own house," because the heart of each one of us is like a house. And so, the pontiff asked himself, "am I the guard of my heart?"

It is indeed necessary "to protect that treasure where the Holy Spirit dwells, so that the other spirits do not enter." And it needs to be done "like one protects a house, with lock and key." After all, the pope said, we use "many types of security" in our houses to defend against thieves. Do we do the same with our heart? Or do we leave "the door open?" One must "be vigilant," Francis advised, because the demon, even though "he has been cast out by baptism, he goes, he finds seven others more evil than himself, and he returns."

Thus constant attention is necessary. One must always ask oneself: "What is happening there," inside us? "Am I the sentry of my heart?" We learn, the pontiff suggested, from our everyday life: "Who among us, when we are at home, whether in the kitchen, or at our desk, wherever we may be, and seeing a person pass through that we don't know, who among us remains calm? No one!" We immediately turn to the stranger: "Who are you? Who let you in? Where did you come in?" The same thing can also happen inside us. "How many times," the bishop of Rome underlined, "do wicked thoughts enter, wicked intentions, jealousy, envy. So many things that enter. But who opened that door? Where did they come in?" And if we are not aware of whom we let into our heart, it "becomes a town square, where everyone comes and goes." You begin to lack intimacy. And there, "the Lord cannot speak or even be heard."

So it happens that, even if our heart "is truly the place to receive the Holy Spirit," without the proper vigilance "the Spirit ends up in a corner," as if we have locked him in "a closet." And there, the Spirit is "sad."

What do we do then, to prevent this occurrence? To answer, the pope took another cue from the gospel. He quoted an expression that Jesus used, "which seems a bit curious: 'he who does not gather with me scatters.'" Starting from the word "gather," Francis explained that one needs "to have a gathered heart," a heart in which we manage to be aware of "what's happening." In this sense, what may be recommended is the age old "but good" practice of examining the conscience. "Who among us," asked the pontiff, "in the evening, before the day is over, is alone" and in the silence "asks himself," What has happened in my heart today? What has occurred? What things have passed through my heart?"

It is an important exercise, a complete "grace" that can help us to be good guardians. Because, the pope recalled, "the devils come back, always, even at the end of life." And to keep watch so the demons do not enter our heart, it is essential to know how to "be in silence before one's self and before God," in order to check whether someone we don't know has entered our house, and whether "the key is in place." This, the pontiff concluded, "helps us to defend ourselves against so much malevolence, also against what we might do ourselves." Because "these demons are so clever" and are capable of misleading everyone.

THE GOD OF SURPRISES

October 13, 2014
GAL 4:22-24, 26-27, 31–5:1; LK 11:29-32

"A heart that loves the law, for the law is God's," but "which also loves God's surprises," for his "holy law is not an end in itself": it is a journey, "a teaching which leads us to Jesus Christ." Pope Francis called us to ask the Lord for this in prayer, during Mass at the Chapel of St. Martha's Guest House.

The pontiff's homily was based mainly on the passage of the gospel according to Luke (11:29-32), in which Jesus harshly criticizes the crowd gathered to hear him as "an evil generation" because "it seeks a sign." According to the bishop of Rome, "it is evident that Jesus is speaking to the doctors of the law," who, "many times in the gospel," ask him for "a sign." Indeed, they "do not see many of Jesus' signs." But this is precisely why "Jesus scolds them" on various occasions: "You are incapable of seeing the signs of the times," he tells them in the gospel of Matthew, drawing upon the image of the fig tree: "as soon as its branch becomes tender and puts forth its leaves, you know that summer is near; and you do not understand the signs of the times."

Pope Francis thus exhorted us to ask ourselves the reason why the doctors of the law did not understand the signs of the times and called for an extraordinary sign. And he proposed several answers: the first was "because they were closed. They were closed within their system; they had organized the law very well." It was "a masterpiece. All of the Jews knew what one could and could not do, where one could go. It was all organized." But Jesus caught them unprepared, by doing "curious things," such as "going with the sinners," and "eating with the publicans." And the doctors of the law did not like this, they found it "dangerous," putting at risk "the doctrine which they, the theologians, had been making for centuries."

In this regard the bishop of Rome acknowledged that it was a law "made for love, in order to be faithful to God," but it had become a closed regulatory system. They "had simply forgotten history. They had forgotten that God is the God of the law," but he is also "the God of surprises. And God, many times, also had surprises in store for his people": suffice it to think of the Red Sea and of "how he saved them" from slavery in Egypt, the pope recalled.

Despite that, however, they "did not understand that God is always new; he never denies himself, he never says that something he had said was a mistake, never; but he always surprises. And they did not understand and they closed themselves within that system created with much good will; and they asked" that Jesus give them "a sign," failing to understand, however, "the many signs that Jesus gave" and maintaining a completely "closed" attitude.

The second response to his initial question, the pontiff pointed out, is attributable to the fact that they "had forgotten that they were a people on a journey. And when one is on a journey one always finds new things, things one does not know. And in the law, they had to accept these things in a heart faithful to the Lord." But, also in this case, "a journey is not absolute in itself, it is a journey toward an end point: toward the definitive manifestation of the Lord." After all, all of "life is a journey toward the fullness of Jesus Christ, when the second coming occurs. It is a journey toward Jesus, who will come again in glory, as the angels said to the apostles on the day of the ascension."

In other words, Pope Francis emphasized, repeating the words from the gospel passage, this generation "seeks a sign, but no sign shall be given to it except the sign of Jonah": that is to say, the pope clarified, "the sign of the resurrection, of glory, of that eschatology we are journeying toward." However, many of his contemporaries "were closed within themselves, not open to the God of surprises"; they were men and women who "did not know the path or even this eschatology, to the point that when, in the Sanhedrin, the priest asks Jesus: 'Tell us if you are the Christ, the Son of God,' and Jesus says, yes, and 'you will see the Son of man seated at the right hand of Power, and coming on the clouds of heaven,' the high priest tore his robes, scandalized. 'He has uttered blasphemy! Blasphemy!' he yelled." For them, the sign that Jesus gave was blasphemy.

For this reason, the pope explained, Jesus defined them as an "evil generation," inasmuch as "they did not understand that the law they protected and loved was a pedagogy toward Jesus Christ." Indeed, "if the law does not lead to Jesus Christ, does not bring us close to Jesus Christ, it is dead." And this is why Jesus scolds the members of that generation "for being closed, for being incapable of recognizing the signs of the times, for not being open to the God of surprises, for not being on a journey toward the Lord's triumphant finale," to the point "that when he explains it, they think it is blasphemy."

The pope then moved on to his final instruction, to reflect on this theme, to ask oneself about these aspects: "Am I attached to my things, to my ideas, closed? Or am I open to the God of surprises?" And also: "Am I a stationary person or a person on a journey?" And finally, he concluded, "do I believe in Jesus Christ and in what he has done?" that is, "he died, rose again . . . do I believe that the journey goes forth toward maturity, toward the manifestation of the glory of the Lord? Am I capable of understanding the signs of the times and of being faithful to the voice of the Lord that is manifest in them?"

APPEARANCE AND TRUTH

October 14, 2014
GAL 5:1-6; LK 11:37-41

"Jesus condemns people with good manners but bad habits," because it is one thing to "appear good and beautiful," but inner truth is something else. In the same way, it isn't good to be bound exclusively to the letter of the law, because "law alone doesn't save. Law saves when it leads you to the source of salvation." During morning Mass at St. Martha's, Pope Francis called for an examination of conscience regarding the state of each Christian's faith.

The day's liturgy offered a reading from the gospel according to Luke (11:37-41), from which the pontiff began his homily. He explained Jesus' attitude with respect to the Pharisee who was scandalized because the Lord did not perform the ritual cleansing before his meal. Christ's response was grim: "You are so concerned with the outside, with appearance, but inside you are filled with plunder and evil." The words go along with those from a parallel passage from Matthew, where he speaks of greed and uncleanness and where the Pharisees are compared to "white-washed tombs, which outwardly appear beautiful, but within they are full of dead men's bones and all uncleanness." In this regard, the pope underscored that Jesus firmly condemned the Pharisees' self-confidence in "having fulfilled the law." He condemned "this cosmetic spirituality."

This refers to the people "who liked to take walks in the town square," and to be seen while they prayed, and to wear a dismal face while they fasted. "Why is the Lord like this?" Francis asked himself, pointing out that, to describe the actions of the Pharisees, the gospel uses two different but related terms: "plunder and evil." He also explained that this evil is "strongly associated with money."

The pontiff then recounted a brief anecdote. "I once heard an elderly preacher of spiritual exercises who said: 'How is sin able to enter the soul? Oh, it's simple! Through your pockets . . .'" Money itself is basically "the door" through which corruption enters the heart. This explains why Jesus stated, "Give for alms those things which are within."

Pope Francis explained that "alms have always been, in the tradition of the Bible, both in the Old and New Testaments, the touchstone of justice. A just man, a just woman is always linked to alms," because with alms we share our own with others, we give what each one "has within."

And thus the Holy Father returned to the theme of appearance and inner truth. The Pharisees whom Jesus speaks of "believed they were good because they did all that the law commanded should be done." But law "alone doesn't save." Law saves "when it leads you to the source of salvation, when it prepares your heart to receive the true salvation that comes from faith."

The same concept, the pope specified, emerges from the day's first reading, taken from the letter of Paul in which he disagrees with the Galatians (5:1-6) because they had been "very attached to the law" and "frightened of the faith" and had "returned to the prescriptions of the law" regarding circumcision. The apostle's words are also well suited to our own daily life, because the faith, the bishop of Rome highlighted, "is not only reciting the Creed: we all believe in the Father, in the Son, and in the Holy Spirit, in life everlasting . . . " But if our faith is "immobile" and "inactive," then "it's of no use."

Thus, what's important in Jesus Christ is "the faith which becomes active in charity." And this brings us back to the theme of alms, intended "in the broadest sense of the word," in other words, "detached from the dictatorship of cash, from the idolatry of money" because "all greed distances us from Jesus Christ."

This is why, the pope explained, throughout the Bible there is "a lot of talk about alms," whether the "small, everyday" alms or the more important ones. It is necessary, though, to pay attention to two things: we mustn't "sound the trumpet when giving alms" and we mustn't limit ourselves to donating only what's extra. It's necessary to "strip oneself" and not give "only the leftovers." It's important to do as that elderly woman did, "who gave all she had to live."

One who gives alms and "sounds the trumpet" so that everyone knows "is not a Christian." This, Francis indicated, is to act as a Pharisee, "it's hypocritical." To better illustrate the concept, the pope told about what happened once to Fr. Pedro Arrupe, the Superior General of the Society of Jesus from 1965 to 1983. In the period that "he was a missionary in Japan," while seeking offerings for his mission, he received an invitation from an important woman who wanted to make a donation. The woman didn't receive him in private, but wanted to consign her envelope in front of "journalists who took photographs." In other words, she "sounded the trumpet."

Fr. Arrupe, recalled the pontiff, said that he had "suffered great humiliation" and had put up with her only for the good of "the poor of Japan, for the mission." Once he returned home, he opened the envelope and discovered that there "were ten dollars" inside. If the heart doesn't change, Pope Francis commented, appearance counts for nothing. And thus concluded his homily. "Today it will do us good to think about how my faith is, how my Christian life is: is it a Christian life of cosmetics, of appearance, or is it a Christian life with a faith which is active in charity?" Everyone can examine his conscience "before God." And "it is good for us to do so."

LIKE BURNING INCENSE

October 16, 2014
EPH 1:1-10; LK 11:47-54

Knowing we were personally chosen even before the creation of the world, every man must rediscover the importance of the free and joyous prayer of praise to God. At Thursday morning's Mass at St. Martha's, Pope Francis chose to reflect on the day's first reading, recalling St. Paul's well-known hymn in the letter to the Ephesians (1:1-10). In this veritable explosion of praise, "it seems that Paul," Francis noted, is overcome with "joy, great joy."

It is an "unrestrained" hymn in which the apostle uses the word "bless" three times: "Blessed be God and Father of our Lord Jesus Christ, who has blessed us in Christ with every spiritual blessing in the heavenly places." But, the pontiff pointed out, "we all know that God is the Blessed One": in the Old Testament, in fact, "it was one of the names that the people of Israel gave him:

the Blessed One." It is curious to think of "blessing God" because "he is the Blessed One."

In truth, it is an important gesture, because "when I bless God, I praise him," and this praise rises "like burning incense." Prayers of praise aren't done habitually, yet, Francis highlighted, it was Jesus himself who taught us, "in the Our Father, to pray this way: Our Father who art in heaven, hallowed be thy name . . . " It shouldn't seem unusual to turn with these words to him who "is the Holy One." It is about expressing the "joy of the prayer of praise," which is "purely free," the bishop of Rome explained. In fact, generally, "we know how to pray extremely well when we ask for things" and also "when we thank the Lord"; it is less customary for all of us "to praise the Lord."

We might feel a stronger incentive toward this type of prayer, the pope advised, if "we remember the things that the Lord has done in our life," as did St. Paul, who recalled in his hymn: "He chose us in him"—in Christ—"before the foundation of the world." Here is the source of our prayer: "Blessed are you, Lord, because you have chosen me!" Man must, so to speak, feel the "joy of paternal and gentle closeness."

The same thing happened to the people of Israel when they were freed from Babylon, the pontiff recalled, citing several verses of Psalm 126[125]: "'When the Lord restored the fortunes of Zion, we were like those who dream'—We couldn't believe it!—'Then our mouth was filled with laughter, and our tongue with shouts of joy.'" And the pope observed: "Let's think of a broad smile; this is a prayer of praise." It is the immediate expression of immense joy, of "being joyful before the Lord." It is the disposition of the heart not to forget: "Let's make an effort to find it again," he urged, calling on us to use the very words of Psalm 98[97]: "Sing praises to the Lord with the lyre, with the lyre and the sound of melody! With trumpets and the sound of the horn, make a joyful noise before the King, the Lord!"

It is very important to remember how much the Lord has done for each one of us, "how he accompanied me with tenderness, how he lowered himself, he bent down" in the same way as a father who "bends down to help his child walk." And, the pope underscored, he has done so "with each one of us."

"All is celebration, all is joy" if each one—as St. Paul himself attests to the Ephesians—can say: "the Lord chose me before the foundation of the world." This is "the starting point." Even if, Francis emphasized, "one can't understand" and "one can't imagine: that the Lord knew me before the creation of the world, that my name was in the Lord's heart." But "this is truth, this is revelation." And, the pontiff added, "if we don't believe this, then we aren't Christians." Perhaps, he explained, "we could be permeated by a theistic religiosity," but we wouldn't be Christians, because precisely this being "chosen" is characteristic of Christians.

The thought of having always lived in the heart of God "fills us with joy" and "gives us security." This security is confirmed by the Lord's words to the prophet Isaiah, who asked himself whether this affection could ever fail: "Can a mother forget her children? And even should a mother forget them I will not forget you." God holds each of us in his "bosom," the way "a baby is inside his mother."

This truth, Francis pointed out, is so great and beautiful that it can be tempting not to think about it, to avoid it as it looms over us. In fact, "it cannot be understood with the mind," and "not even with the heart." To make it our own and to experience it, he explained, "we must enter into the mystery of Jesus Christ," of him who "so freely shed his blood for us," and who "has made known to us in all wisdom and insight the mystery of his will."

Hence the third fundamental approach of the Christian, after those of the prayer of praise and of knowing how to remember. The Christian is called "to enter into the mystery" above all when "we celebrate the Eucharist," as we are unable to fully comprehend "that the Lord is alive; he is with us, here, in his glory, his fullness, and he gives his life for us once again."

It is an approach, the pontiff concluded, that we must make an effort to "learn every day" because "the mystery can't be controlled: it's a mystery! We must enter it."

Where Heaven Begins

October 17, 2014
Eph 1:11-14; Lk 12:1-7

A Christian cannot allow himself "to be lukewarm": he has a specific identity which was given by the seal of the Holy Spirit. During Mass at St. Martha's on Friday, Pope Francis turned his reflection to the beginning of the letter of Paul to the Ephesians and on Christians "chosen by the Lord before the creation of the world." Among those present in the chapel was Shoah survivor Enzo Camerino, who had previously met the pontiff on October 16, 2013, on the 70th anniversary of the raid on the ghetto of Rome.

The Lord, the pontiff said, recalling the words of St. Paul, "not only chose us" but also "gave us an identity." And, Francis explained, we did not inherit merely a name, "but an identity, a way of life, which is not only a list of customs, it's more: it's an actual identity." And how have we been "marked" so deeply? The apostle writes: you have been "sealed with the Holy Spirit." Our identity, the bishop of Rome stated, "is this very seal, this power of the Holy Spirit, which we have all received in baptism."

And since the Holy Spirit had been promised to us by Jesus, "He sealed our heart" and, what's more, he "walks with us." He not only gives us an identity, but it is also the "guarantee of our inheritance. Heaven begins there." A Christian thus acts in earthly life but is already living from the perspective of "eternity." Pope Francis further emphasized: "With this seal we have Heaven in our grasp."

Everyday life is sprinkled with temptations, first of all, with that of "not realizing this beauty that we've received." When this happens, the Spirit, to use an expression of Paul's, "grieves": this happens, the Holy Father underlined, not when we want "to erase the identity, but to render it opaque." This is the case of the "lukewarm Christian," the one who "goes to Mass on Sunday, yes, but the identity isn't seen in his life"; the one who, despite being a Christian, "lives like a pagan." Then there is another risk, the other sin "which Jesus speaks to the disciples about" when he tells them: "Beware of the leaven of the Pharisees, which is hypocrisy." It happens, the pope recalled, that some "pretend to be Christians," those who lack "transparency" in their actions, who profess one thing in words but act differently in fact. "And this," he added, "is what the doctors of the law did"; it is the leaven of "hypocrisy" which risks growing inside us.

Rendering our identity opaque and betraying it in our actions are "two sins against this seal" which "is a beautiful gift of God, the Spirit" and is the "guarantee of what awaits us," of what "we have been promised." This is why we are able to say that "we have Heaven in our grasp."

What, then, the pontiff asked, is "the true conduct of a Christian?" We learn it from Paul himself: "The fruit of the Spirit, which comes from our identity, is love, joy, peace, magnanimity, good will, goodness, faithfulness, meekness, self-control." And this, Pope Francis concluded, is "our road toward heaven."

WAITING WITH HOPE

October 21, 2014
EPH 2:12-22; LK 12:35-38

Christians are called to be men and women of hope, united by the certainty of a God who does not give up. This was part of the message of Pope Francis' homily during Mass at St. Martha's on Tuesday morning.

Looking at the day's reading from the gospel of Luke (12:35-38), in which Jesus calls on his disciples to be as servants, vigilant and awaiting the master's return from a wedding, the pontiff asked: "Who is this lord, this master, who is coming home from a marriage feast, who is coming late at night?" The answer comes from Jesus himself: "It is I who have come to serve you, to gird my loins, to seat you at the table, to serve you."

St. Paul, too, in the letter to the Ephesians (2:12-22), reiterates that it is Jesus who has "come to serve, not to be served." And the first gift that we received from him is that of an identity. Jesus has given us "citizenship, membership in a commonwealth, a first and last name." Taking up the words of the apostle, who reminds the pagans that when they were separated from Christ they were "alienated from the commonwealth," Francis highlighted: "Without Christ we have no identity."

Thanks to him, indeed, once separated we have become one "people." We were "enemies, without peace," isolated, but Jesus, "united us with his blood." This theme also comes from St. Paul, who writes in the letter to the Ephesians: "For he is our peace, who has made us both one, and has broken down the dividing wall." We all know, the bishop of Rome recalled, that "when we are not at peace with people, there is a wall that divides us." But Jesus "offers us his service to knock down this wall." Thanks to him "we are able to meet each other."

From a people broken apart, comprised of men isolated from one another, Jesus, with his service, "has brought everyone near, has made us one body." And he has reconciled everyone in God. Thus, "from enemies" we have become "friends," and from "strangers" we can now feel we are "children."

"But what is the condition" through which from "strangers," from "sojourners" we are able to become "fellow citizens with the saints"? To have confidence, the pope answered, in the master's return from the wedding feast, in Jesus. It is necessary to "await him" and to be ever ready: "Those who do not await Jesus close the door to Jesus, don't allow him to do this work of peace, of community, of citizenship; moreover: of name." That name that reminds us who we truly are: "children of God."

This is why "a Christian is a man or a woman of hope," because he or she "knows that the Lord will come." And when this happens, although "we don't know when," no longer will "we find ourselves isolated, enemies," but rather as he, through his service, has made us: "friends, neighbors, at peace."

For this reason, Pope Francis concluded, it is important to ask ourselves: "How do I await Jesus?" But above all: "Do I or do I not await" Jesus? Many times, in fact, even we Christians "behave like pagans" and "live as if nothing could happen." We must be careful not to be like a "selfish pagan," who acts as though he himself "were a king" and thinks: "I can manage on my own." Those who behave in this manner come to no good, end up nameless, with no one close, without citizenship. Each one of us must instead ask ourselves: "Do I believe in this hope, that he will come?" And: "Do I have an open heart to hear the sound, when he knocks at the door, when he opens the door?"

An Infinite Horizon

October 23, 2014
Eph 3:14-21; Lk 12:49-53

Paul's "mystical experience" with Jesus reminds us that alone we cannot be Christians, loving God and our neighbor "without the power and grace of the Holy Spirit." In his homily on Thursday during Mass at St. Martha's, Pope Francis offered the experience of Paul the apostle as an example of prayers of adoration and praise.

"Paul has an experience with Jesus, an experience with the Lord, which leads him to leave everything," to the point of saying that he "has given up everything and considers everything rubbish, in order to receive Christ and to be found in him." In fact, he "saw Christ, he met Christ, and fell in love with Christ." And he "goes forth in this mystery." Thus, from the day's first reading from the letter to the Ephesians (3:14-21), the pontiff pointed out: "we listened to that act of adoration that Paul makes before God: Brethren, 'I kneel before the Father.'" This is his act of adoration to the Father, and "then he explains the reason to us."

The passage from the day's liturgy, Francis stated, "is original in the language that Paul uses." It is, in fact, "a timeless language, a grandiose, expansive language: he speaks of the riches of his glory; he speaks of comprehending the breadth, the length, the height, the depth; to know the Christ who surpasses, the Christ who causes us to be filled with all fullness." And it is indeed "timeless language, incapable of being understood in the sense of comprehending," because it is "almost without a horizon."

Paul "adores this God who is able to accomplish far more than all we ask or imagine, according to that power that he has even in time, for all generations, for ever and ever." It is an outright "act of adoration, an experience before this God who is as a sea without shores, without limits, an immense ocean." And "Paul's heart, his soul, kneel before God."

"In this act of adoration," the pope affirmed, "Paul tells us of the Father, of the Son, and of the Holy Spirit." And "what does Paul ask, for himself, for the church—in this case the church of Ephesus—and for all of us?" Turning to "the Father, from whom every family in heaven and on earth is named," Paul asks first "to be strengthened with power through his Spirit in the inner self." Beyond this he asks "the Father that the Spirit come and strengthen us, give us strength." He knows well that "one cannot go forward without the Spirit's power. Our strength is weak. One cannot be a Christian without the grace of the Spirit." Indeed, "it is precisely the Spirit who changes our heart, who enables us to go forward in virtue in order to fulfill the commandments."

Then, Paul "asks for another grace of God, but through Christ: that Christ may dwell in your hearts through faith," and thus be "rooted and grounded in love." He basically "asks for the presence of Christ, that he may make us grow in charity, but rooted in love, grounded in love." And also, he asks the Father for the ability "to comprehend . . . the love of Christ which surpasses knowledge," which is beyond comprehension. But then, "how can I understand what is beyond comprehension?" Paul's answer is clear: "Through this act of adoration of that great immensity."

In the passage from the letter to the Ephesians, Paul continues speaking "to the faithful about the Father: he began with the Father and ended with the Father." Thus, he speaks directly to the faithful about "him who in all things has the power to act." The apostle affirms that the Father is able to do "far more than all we ask or imagine." Even miracles, of course. "But we cannot imagine what the Father can do by the power at work within us." Paul then ends this adoration with praise: "to him be glory forever and ever."

Before us, Francis explained, is the "mystical experience of Paul, who teaches us the prayer of praise and the prayer of adoration." Thus, "before our smallness, our selfish interests—so many!—Paul bursts out in this praise, in this act of adoration." And he "asks the Father to send us the Spirit to give us the strength and power to go forward; that he enable us to comprehend the love of Christ and that Christ strengthen us in love." And he says to the Father: "Thank you, because you are able to do what we do not even dare to imagine."

This "is a beautiful prayer" of Paul's, the pope commented. And "with this interior life one can understand that Paul has given up everything and considers everything rubbish, in order to receive Christ and to be found in Christ." His words also apply to us today because "it's good for us to think this way; it's good for us, too, to praise God." Yes, "it does us good to praise God, to enter into this expansive world of grandeur, of generosity, and of love." And, Francis concluded, "it does us good because in this way we are able to go forward in the great commandment—the one commandment that is the basis of all the others—which is love: love God and love your neighbor."

STONES AND BRICKS

October 24, 2014
EPH 4:1-6; LK 12:54-59

It is the Holy Spirit who builds the church and cements her unity, founded on the cornerstone that is Jesus. To guide our collaboration in this construction, we have a "floor plan," which we call hope, and one instruction: we must be weak in order to be strong. These spiritual suggestions of St. Paul were highlighted by Pope Francis on Friday, during morning Mass at St. Martha's.

The Holy Father focused immediately on the word "one" as "the word most repeated by the apostle Paul in the passage from the letter to the Ephesians" (4:1-6) offered in the day's liturgy. Indeed, it reads: "one Lord, one faith, one baptism, one God and Father of all." Yes, the word "one" is repeated many times. And in just this perspective, Paul writes explicitly: "I, a prisoner, beg you to build unity in the church." Paul's exhortation, Francis explained, is aimed at building "the church united, with one baptism, one faith, one Lord, one Father." And "it is the work of the church and of every Christian throughout history to build the unity of the church."

In particular, the pope stated, when "the apostle Peter speaks of the church, he speaks of a temple made of living stones, which are us." Essentially, Peter proposes "the opposite of the other temple of arrogance, which is the Tower of Babel." In fact "this temple leads to unity," while that of Babel "is the symbol of disunity, of not understanding, of diversity of languages."

Therefore, the pope stated, "building the unity of the church, constructing the church, this temple, this unity of the church, is the task of every Christian, of each one of us." And, "when we need to build a temple, a building, we look for a building site prepared for this." But "the first thing we do is to look for a foundation stone: the cornerstone, the Bible says." And "the cornerstone of the church is Jesus," while "the cornerstone of the church's unity is Jesus' prayer at the Last Supper: Father, that they may be one." This, the bishop of Rome said, is "the strength" and "the stone upon which we build the unity of the church. Without this stone it isn't possible. There isn't unity without Jesus Christ at the foundation: He is our security."

But, asked Francis, "who builds this unity?" Certainly not us, he emphasized, because "this is the work of the Holy Spirit: the only one capable of building the unity of the church." Jesus, in fact, "sent him to make the church grow, to make her strong, to make her one." It is "the living Spirit that we all have inside: He creates the unity of the church, in the diversity of nations, of cultures, of people." Precisely "in that diversity he knows how to create unity. But only he can do it; none of us can."

Francis then posed another question: "How do we build this temple?" In this regard, the apostle Peter "said that we were living stones in this building." But, the pontiff noted, "here, the apostle Peter advises us not to be stones but, rather, bricks, weak ones." As a result, "the counsel that Paul gives in order to help the Holy Spirit build this unity is the advice of weakness, according to human thought." And indeed, "humility, gentleness, magnanimity are weaknesses, because humility doesn't seem to be helpful for anything; gentleness, meekness aren't useful; magnanimity, being open to everyone, to have a big heart . . ."

Moreover, Paul adds: "bearing with one another through love," but "striving to serve the unity." Therefore, "we become stronger stones in this temple, the weaker we are with these virtues of humility, of magnanimity, of gentleness, of meekness."

And it is exactly "the same path" taken by Jesus, who "doesn't claim to be God's equal. He lowers himself, he abases himself, he weakens himself, weak, weak until the cross, and he becomes strong." The pope recalled that we are called to do "the same: the more we are bricks, thus with these virtues, the more helpful we will be to the Holy Spirit in building the unity of the church." On the other hand, "pride, arrogance aren't useful."

In the end it can be said, the pope remarked, that "it is the Holy Spirit who creates this building, this temple that is the living church, on the cornerstone that is Jesus, who is one; on the cornerstone that is Jesus' prayer for unity." But Paul adds one other thing: "One body and one Spirit, as you were also called to the one hope of your calling." Because "when we construct a building, it is necessary for an architect to draw the floor plan." And "what is the church's floor plan? The hope to which we have been called: the hope to go toward the Lord, the hope of living in one living church, built with living stones, with the power of the Holy Spirit." For this reason, "only according to the floor plan of hope can we go forward in the unity of the church."

Francis concluded by recalling that "we have been called to great hope"; and thus, he urged, "let us go there." But let's do so "with the strength given us by Jesus' prayer for unity and with docility to the Holy Spirit, who is capable of making living stones from bricks." And also "with the hope of finding the Lord who has called us, to find him in the fullness of time."

CHRISTIANS IN A GRAY AREA

October 27, 2014
EPH 4:32–5:8; LK 13:10-17

An examination of conscience regarding our words, as St. Paul proposes, will help us to answer an essential question about ourselves: Are we Christians of light, of darkness, or worse: are we gray Christians? Pope Francis asked this question during Mass at St. Martha's on Monday morning, October 27.

As his point of departure for this essential examination of conscience, the Holy Father turned to the letter to the Ephesians (4:32–5:8): "St. Paul says to the Christians that we must behave as children of light and not as children of darkness, as we once were." And "to explain this, both he and the gospel (Lk 13:10-17) offer a catechesis on language: what is the speech of a child of light and what is the speech of a child of darkness."

Thus, the pope explained, beginning the Pauline catechesis, "the speech of a child who is not of light might be obscene words, vulgar words." Indeed, the apostle says: "But immorality and all impurity or covetousness must not even be named among you" (Eph 5:3).

And thus, Francis pointed out, "a child of light doesn't have this vulgar language, this dirty language."

There is, however, "a second kind of speech, a worldly speech." Such that Paul suggests that "filthiness, nor silly talk, nor triviality" should even be spoken. And "worldliness is vulgar and trivial," the pope remarked. On his part, "a child of light isn't worldly and mustn't speak of worldliness, of vulgarity."

But St. Paul goes further and says: "Be careful, let no one deceive you with empty words." Since this message is still quite relevant today, the pontiff immediately added, with regard to empty words: "we hear a lot of them." And some of them are even "beautiful, well spoken, but empty, with nothing behind them." For this reason, "not even this is the language of the child of light."

Still, Francis stated, "there is another word of the gospel" and it is exactly "the one that Jesus says to the doctors of the law: 'Hypocrites.'" Yes, the very word, "hypocrite." The pope explained that we, too, "might think about how our speech is: is it hypocritical? Is it a little here and a little there, in order to be okay with everyone? Is it empty speech, without substance, full of vacuity? Is it vulgar, trivial, that is, worldly speech? Is it dirty, obscene speech?" St. Paul says clearly, the bishop of Rome explained, that these four types of speech "don't belong to children of light; they don't come from the Holy Spirit, they don't come from Jesus," they don't come from the gospel. Therefore, "this way of speaking, always talking about dirty or worldly or vacuous things or speaking hypocritically," isn't befitting children of light. On the other hand, "what is the speech of saints, that is, the language of a child of light?" The answer again comes from Paul: "Be imitators of God, walk in love; walk in goodness; walk in docility." Those who walk like this are children of light. And moreover, "Be tenderhearted," Paul says, "forgiving one another, as God in Christ forgave you. Therefore be imitators of God" and "walk in love."

In substance, this exhortation invites us to walk in "mercy, in forgiveness, in charity." This is precisely "the speech of a child of light," Francis affirmed, as he left the letter to the Ephesians.

"Today the church leads us to reflect on the way of speaking and from this she will help us to understand whether we are children of light or children of darkness," the pope indicated. He then provided guidance in practical points of reference: "Remember: no obscene language! No vulgar and worldly words! No vacuous words! No hypocritical words!" These types of speech, in fact, "do not belong to God, they belong to the Evil One."

It's true, the pontiff related, that we can really understand and recognize the differences between children of light and children of darkness. "Children of light shine," as Jesus says to his disciples: "May your works shine and give glory to the Father." It is an obvious fact that "the light shines and illuminates others on the path." And "there are luminous Christians, full of light, who seek

to serve the Lord with this light." As on the other side, "there are
dark Christians, who want nothing from the Lord and who lead
a life of sin, a life far away from the Lord." And these Christians
use the four types of speech that Paul indicated.

However, not everything is always so clear and recognizable:
on one hand the children of darkness and on the other the children of light. "There is a third group of Christians," Pope Francis explained, "that is the most difficult and complex of all: the
neither light nor dark Christians." And these "are Christians in
a gray area," who "are on this side one time, and on the other" at
another time, such that, speaking of them, people say, "Is this person okay with God or with the Devil?" And they say this because
these Christians are "always in a gray area: they are lukewarm"
and "they are neither luminous nor dark."

But "God doesn't love these ones." We read this in Revelation
when "the Lord says to these Christians of grayness, 'you are neither cold nor hot. Would that you were cold or hot! So, because
you are lukewarm—gray—I will spew you out of my mouth!'"

So, the pope said, "the Lord is harsh with gray Christians."
And it's no use justifying in self-defense, "I am a Christian, but I
don't overdo it."

These gray people, in fact, "do a lot of harm, because their
Christian testimony is a testimony that, in the end, sows confusion, sows a negative testament." And Paul is particularly clear in
this regard: "once you were darkness, but now you are light in the
Lord. Walk as children of light." Paul says "children of light" and
"not children of darkness, not children of grayness."

The passage of St. Paul, Francis concluded, is a good ther-
mometer for reconsidering "our language." And it may be helpful to answer these questions: "How do we speak? Which of
these four [types of] words do we speak with? Obscene words,
worldly, vulgar words, vacuous words, hypocritical words?" And
the answer to these questions, the pope added, should suggest

another question: "Am I a Christian of light? Am I a Christian of darkness? Am I a Christian of grayness?" This practical examination of conscience will help us "to take a step forward, to encounter the Lord."

CATHOLIC, BUT NOT TOO CATHOLIC

October 28, 2014
EPH 2:19-22; LK 6:12-16

There are Christians who stop at the "reception desk" of the church and linger at the threshold, without going in, to avoid compromising themselves. This is the approach of those who say they are "Catholic, but" not too Catholic. Pope Francis spoke of them during morning Mass at St. Martha's on Tuesday.

On the feast day of the apostles Sts. Simon and Jude, the pontiff pointed out that "the church causes us to reflect on her," inviting us to consider "how the church is" and "what the church is." In the letter to the Ephesians (2:19-22), "the first thing that Paul tells us is that we are neither strangers nor sojourners: we are not passing through, in this city that is the church, but we are fellow citizens." Thus, "the Lord calls us to his church with the rights of a citizen; we are not passing through, we are rooted there. Our life is there."

And Paul "makes an icon of the building of the temple," writing, "built upon the foundation of the apostles and prophets, Christ Jesus himself being the cornerstone." Exactly "this is the church," the pope confirmed. For we "are built upon the pillars of the apostles. The cornerstone, the foundation, is Christ Jesus himself, and we are inside."

St. Paul continues, explaining that in Christ "the whole structure is joined together and grows into a holy temple in the Lord. In him you also are built to be a dwelling place of God through the Spirit." This, then, is "the definition of the church that Paul gives us today: a temple built." And thus, "we too are built to become a dwelling place of the Spirit": we are "built," Francis indicated, "upon the pillars of the apostles and upon this cornerstone that is Jesus Christ."

The pontiff then indicated that "we are also able to see" this same vision of the church "developed a bit in the passage of the gospel" according to Luke (6:12-19), which tells how Jesus chose the apostles. The evangelist "says that Jesus went into the hills to pray. And then he called these twelve; he chose them." Then Jesus came down with them from the hills and found on a level place, waiting for him, "a great crowd of his disciples, whom he would send out" and "a great multitude of people who sought to touch him" in order to be healed.

In other words, the pope explained, "Jesus prays, Jesus calls, Jesus chooses, Jesus sends out his disciples, Jesus heals the crowd." And "within this temple, Jesus, who is the cornerstone, does all this work: it is he who leads the church forward in this way." Just as Paul writes, "this church is built upon the foundation of the apostles whom he chose." This is confirmed by the gospel passage, which tells that the Lord "chose from them twelve: all sinners, all." Judas, the bishop of Rome observed, "wasn't the most sinful," and "I don't know who was the most sinful." But "poor Judas is that one who closed himself to love and this is why he became a traitor." The fact remains that "all of the apostles fled at the difficult moment of the Passion, and they left Jesus alone: all are sinners." But nevertheless, Jesus himself chose them.

Thus, Francis continued, "Jesus creates the church through his prayer; he does so through the selection of the apostles; he does so through the choice of the disciples whom he then sends out; he does so through the encounter with the people." Jesus is never "separated from the people. He is always in the midst of the crowd who seeks to touch him, 'for power came forth from him and healed them all,'" as Luke highlights in his gospel.

"We are citizens, fellow citizens of this church," the pope pointed out. For this reason, "if we do not enter this temple and become part of this construction in order that the Holy Spirit may dwell in us, we are not in the church." We are rather, watching "from the threshold," perhaps saying: "How beautiful, yes, this is beautiful!" And this way, we end up being "Christians who go no further than the 'reception desk' of the church. They are there, at the threshold," with the attitude of one who thinks: "well yes, I'm Catholic, but" not too Catholic!

According to Francis, "perhaps the most beautiful thing one can say about how the church is built is the first and last word of the gospel passage: 'Jesus prays,' he 'went out into the hills to pray; and all night he continued in prayer to God.'" Thus, "Jesus prays and Jesus heals," precisely because "power came forth from him and healed them all." Precisely "within this framework—Jesus prays and Jesus heals—there is all that one can say about the church: Jesus who prays for his own, for the pillars, for the disciples, for his people; and Jesus who heals, who accommodates the people, who bestows health of soul and body."

In this regard, the pope repeated Jesus' dialogue with Peter, "the pillar." The Lord "chose him, in that moment" and reassured him, telling him: "I prayed for you, in order that your faith not diminish." It is Jesus who prays for Peter. "This dialogue," the pope stated, "ends after Peter denies Jesus." And therefore, the Lord asks him, by the Sea of Tiberias, "Peter, do you love me more than these?"

This dialogue shows, the pontiff explained, "Jesus who prays and Jesus who heals Peter's heart, wounded by betrayal." And even so, "he makes a pillar of him." This means that "Peter's sin doesn't matter to Jesus; he seeks the heart." But "in order to find this heart, and to heal it, he prayed."

The reality of "Jesus who prays and Jesus who heals" applies even today, for all of us. Because, the pope emphasized, "we cannot comprehend the church without this Jesus who prays and this Jesus who heals." And Francis then concluded his meditation by praying to the Holy Spirit, that "he enable us all to understand this church which has power in Jesus' prayer for us and which is capable of healing us all."

A Beautiful Struggle

October 30, 2014
Eph 6:10-20; Lk 13:31-45

The life of a Christian "is a military life" and it takes "strength and courage" to "withstand" the devil's temptations and to "proclaim" the truth. This "is a beautiful battle" because "when the Lord prevails in every step of our life, it gives us joy, a great happiness." During Thursday's Mass at St. Martha's, reflecting on Paul's words in the letter to the Ephesians (6:10-20) and on his "military language," Pope Francis referred to what theologians call "spiritual warfare," advising that "to pursue a spiritual life, you have to fight."

It takes "strength and courage," the pontiff explained, for it is not a "simple confrontation" but a "continuous battle" with the "Prince of Darkness." It is this close confrontation, the pope indicated, which is referred to in the catechism in which "they taught us that in Christian life there are three enemies: the demon, the world, and the flesh." It's about the everyday struggle with "greed, lust, gluttony, arrogance, pride, envy": all vices "which are the wound of original sin."

We could ask ourselves, "Is the salvation that Jesus gives us free?" Yes, Francis answered, "but you have to protect it!" And as Paul writes, to do so we have to "put on the whole armor of God" for "one cannot think of a spiritual life, a Christian life" without "withstanding temptations, without battling the devil."

And to think, Francis stated, they wanted us to believe "that the devil was a myth, a figure, an idea, the idea of evil." However, "the devil exists and we have to fight against him." St. Paul recalls it, "the word of God says it," yet it seems that "we aren't quite convinced" of this reality.

How is this "armor of God" made? The apostle provides a few details: "Stand, therefore, having girded your loins with truth." Thus, first of all, truth is required because "the devil is a liar; he is the father of liars." Then, Paul continues, one must put on "the breastplate of righteousness"; indeed, the bishop of Rome explained, "we cannot be Christians without continuously working to be just."

And also: "having shod your feet with the equipment of the gospel of peace." In fact, "a Christian is a man or a woman of peace," and if there isn't "peace in the heart" then there's something wrong: it's peace that "gives you strength for the battle."

In the end, the letter to the Ephesians reads: "above all taking the shield of faith." The pontiff paused on this detail: "One thing that would really help us would be to ask ourselves: "How is my faith? Do I believe or not? Or do I partly believe and partly not? Am I somewhat worldly and somewhat a believer?" When we recite the Creed, do we do so only in "words"? Are we aware, Francis asked, that "without faith we can't go forward, we can't safeguard the salvation of God?"

Recalling a passage from chapter nine of the gospel of John, in which Jesus heals the young man who the Pharisees did not believe was blind, Pope Francis pointed out that Jesus doesn't ask the young man, "Are you glad? Are you happy? Have you seen that I am good?" but rather: "Do you believe in the Son of Man? Do you have faith?" And every day, he asks us the same inescapable question, because "if our faith is weak, the devil will defeat us."

The shield of faith not only "protects us, but it also gives us life." And with this, Paul says, we are able "to quench all the flaming darts of the evil one." The devil, in fact, "doesn't cast flowers on us" but "flaming, poisonous arrows."

The armor of a Christian, the pope continued, also includes the "helmet of salvation," the "sword of the Spirit," and prayer. St. Paul advises: "Pray at all times," and the pontiff repeated: "Pray, pray." One cannot "pursue a Christian life without vigilance."

This is why Christian life can be considered a military life. But, the pope stated, it is "a beautiful struggle," because it gives us "that joy that the Lord has prevailed within us, with his freely given salvation." Yet, Francis concluded, we are all "a bit lazy" and "we allow ourselves to be led by vices, by certain temptations." But although "we are sinners," we mustn't get discouraged, "because the Lord is with us, who has given us everything," and he will lead us "to even win today's little pass," our everyday battle.

THE LAW AND THE FLESH

October 31, 2014
PHIL 1:1-11; LK 14:1-6

There are "two paths," and it is Jesus himself, with his "gestures of closeness," who tells us which direction to take. One, indeed, is the path of the "hypocrites," who close doors by sticking to the "letter of the law." On the other, however, is "the path of charity," which passes "from love to the true justice that is within the law." These were the words of Pope Francis as he celebrated Mass at St. Martha's on Friday morning.

To present these two ways of living, the pontiff referred to a passage from the gospel according to Luke (14:1-6). One Sabbath, he recalled, "Jesus was at the home of one of the Pharisee leaders to dine with them; and they were watching him to see what he would do." Most of all, the pope pointed out, "they were trying to catch him in a mistake, even baiting him."

At this point, a sick man enters the scene. Jesus turns to the Pharisees and asks, "Is it lawful to heal on the Sabbath?" as if to say, "Is it lawful to do good on the Sabbath? Or shouldn't I?" Jesus' question, the pope added, is "a simple question but, like all hypocrites, they kept quiet; they didn't say anything." After all, Francis said, "they always fell silent" when Jesus confronted them with the truth, they "kept their mouths shut"; and "they then talked behind his back" and tried to bring him down.

Essentially, the pontiff stated, "these people were so attached to the law that they forgot about justice, so stuck to the law that they forgot about love." But "not only to the law, they stuck to the words, to the letter of the law." This is why "Jesus reproached them," deploring their attitude: "If you, before the needs of your elderly parents, say: 'Dear parents, I love you so much but I can't help you because I gave everything to the temple,' which is more important? The fourth commandment or the temple?"

This very way "of living, attached to the law, distanced them from love and from justice: they were attentive to the law, they disregarded justice; they were attentive to the law, they overlooked love." Yet "they were the models." Jesus, however, "finds only one word" for these people: "hypocrite." One cannot go "around the world seeking converts" and then close "the door."

The Lord found these were "closed men, men too attached to the law," or rather, too attached "to the letter of the law," because "the law is love." These men "always closed the doors of hope, of love, of salvation." They were "men who only knew how to close."

We must ask ourselves, "What is the way to be faithful to the law without overlooking justice, without neglecting love?" The answer "is the very way that comes from the opposite" side, Francis said, repeating Paul's words in the letter to the Philippians (1:1-11): "And it is my prayer that your love may abound more and more, with knowledge and all discernment, so that you may approve what is excellent, and may be pure and blameless."

It is indeed "the opposite path, from love to integrity; from love to discernment; from love to the law." Paul, in fact, prays "that your charity, your love, your works of charity bring you to knowledge and to full discernment." This is precisely "the path that Jesus teaches us, the exact opposite of that of the doctors of the law." And "this path, from love to justice, leads to God." Only "the path that goes from love to knowledge and to discernment, to complete fulfillment, leads to holiness, to salvation, to the encounter with Jesus."

"The other path," however, "that of sticking only to the law, to the letter of the law, leads to closure, leads to selfishness." And it leads "to the arrogance of considering ourselves just," to that so-called "'holiness' of appearances." Such that "Jesus says to these people: you like people to see you as men of prayer, of fasting." This is only for appearances. And "this is why Jesus said to the people: do what they say, not what they do," because "that mustn't be done."

See, then, "the two paths" that we have before us. And with "small gestures," Jesus makes us understand which is the path that goes "from love to full knowledge and to discernment."

Luke presents one of these gestures in the gospel passage from the day's liturgy: "Jesus had this man before him, ill, and when the Pharisees didn't answer, what did Jesus do?" According to the evangelist, "He took him by the hand and healed him, and then he let him go." Thus, first "Jesus draws near: closeness is the very proof" that we are "on the true path." Because that is "the path that God has chosen in order to save us: closeness. He drew close to us, he made himself man." And indeed, "God's flesh is the sign; God's flesh is the sign of true justice. God who made himself a man like one of us, and we who must make ourselves like the others, like the needy, like those who need our help."

Francis also pointed out how "beautiful" is Jesus' gesture of taking a sick person "by the hand." He also does this with "that young man" who had died, "the widow's son, in Nain"; just as "he does with the girl, the daughter of Jairus"; and again with "the boy, the one who had many demons, when he takes him and he gives him to his father." Jesus always takes people "by the hand, because he draws near." And "Jesus' flesh, this closeness, is the bridge that brings us close to God."

This "is not the letter of the law." Only "in the flesh of Christ," in fact, does the law have "complete fulfillment." Because "the flesh of Christ knows how to suffer, he gave his life for us." Meanwhile, "the letter is cold."

Here, then, are the "two paths." The first belongs to those who say: "I stick to the letter of the law; you can't heal on the Sabbath; I can't help; I have to go home and I can't help this sick person." The second is that of those who commit to acting in a way, as Paul writes, "that your love may abound more and more, with knowledge and full discernment": this is "the path of charity, from love to the true justice that is within the law." To help us are these very "examples of Jesus' closeness," which show us how to pass "from love to the fulfillment of the law," without "ever slipping into hypocrisy," because "a Christian hypocrite is too ugly."

WHAT IS A BISHOP'S JOY?

November 3, 2014
PHIL 2:1-4; LK 14:12-14

"A bishop's feelings" or "a bishop's joy." Pope Francis himself provided the ideal title for the passage from the reading from the letter of St. Paul to the Philippians (2:1-4) on Monday, November 3. He also warned about the rivalry and conceit that undermine the life of the church, where it is instead necessary to treasure the directions given by Jesus and Paul: not to seek one's own interests but to humbly serve others while asking for nothing in return. This was the theme of the Holy Father's morning Mass at St. Martha's Guest House.

Paul develops this practical advice, the pontiff explained, in a text which shows "his feelings toward the Philippians. Perhaps the church of the Philippians was the one he loved the most." And "he begins as if asking a favor." Indeed, he writes: "if there is any encouragement, any incentive of love, any participation in the Spirit, any affection and sympathy," in other words, "if you are this way, do me this favor: complete my joy."

Thus, Paul specifically asks the Philippians to "complete the bishop's joy." And "what is the joy of a bishop? What is the joy that Paul asks of the church of the Philippians?" The answer is "to have the same feeling with the same love, being in unanimous agreement." Look, "Paul, as a pastor, knows that this is the path of Jesus. And also that this is the grace that Jesus, in prayer after the Last Supper, asked of the Father: unity, harmony; that the disciples would remain unanimous in agreement with the same love and the same feeling, that is, the harmony of the church."

"We all know," Francis explained, "that this harmony is a grace. The Holy Spirit creates it, but we must, for our part, do everything to help the Holy Spirit in order to build this harmony in the church"; and also "in order to help understand what he asks of the church." The Spirit, in fact, "gives advice, so to speak, in a negative way, that is: 'don't do this, don't do that!'" And "what mustn't the Philippians do?" According to Paul: "Do nothing from rivalry or conceit." This is how, Pope Francis noted, "we can see that this isn't only something of our time," but "it comes from long ago."

Thus Paul recommends not to do anything out of "rivalry," and "not to fight against one another," or even to show off, in order to give the air of being better than others." The bishop of Rome noted further that so often "in our institutions, in the church, in the parishes, for example, in the colleges, we find rivalry, showing off, conceit." It is like "two worms eating away at the consistency of the church, making her weak. Rivalry and conceit work against this harmony, this concordance."

To avoid falling into these temptations, "what does Paul advise?" He writes to the Philippians: "Each of you, in all humility—what must you do in humility?—consider others superior to yourself." Paul "feels this," so that "he qualifies himself unworthy to be called an apostle." He defines himself "the least" and thus "he also forcefully humbles himself." This is "his feeling: thinking that others are superior to him."

Along the same line, Francis recalled the testimony of St. Martino de Porres, a humble Peruvian Dominican Brother, whose liturgical memorial falls on November 3. "His spirituality was in service because he felt that all others, even the worst sinners, were superior to him. He truly felt this." What's more, "he lived this way" and with such "humility" in a time very close to our own.

Thus, the pope indicated that "a bishop's joy is this unity of the church: humility without rivalry or conceit." And Paul then continues: "Let each of you look not only to his own interests, but also to the interests of others." It is thus necessary "to seek good" for others, "to serve others." Because "this is the joy of a bishop when he sees his church like this: the same feeling, the same love, being in unanimous agreement." And "this is the air that Jesus wants in the church. We can have different opinions, okay! But always in this air, this atmosphere of humility, love, without scorning anyone."

Paul's clear recommendation is "not to seek your own interest" alone, but "also that of others." Therefore, he exhorts us not to "try to take advantage for ourselves," looking out exclusively for our own interests. And, Francis said, "it is terrible when, in institutions of the church, of a diocese, we find in parishes people who seek their own interests, not service, not love." And Jesus, too, "tells us in the gospel: do not seek your own interests, do not go down the path of even exchange, of quid pro quo." In other words, don't say, "Yes, I did you this favor, so you do this for me." Jesus recalls this in the gospel of Luke (14:12-14) with the parable that tells of the dinner invitation to "those who are unable to repay: this is gratuity."

"When in a church," the pontiff emphasized, "there is harmony, there is unity, we don't seek our own interests, this is the attitude of gratuity." This way "I do good," I don't "bargain with good." There is also, on the other hand, a "tendency toward utilitarianism." However, "the love which Paul asks for rejects utilitarianism: do good, be humble toward others who in your heart you consider better than you."

Francis recommended that we think throughout the day about "what my parish is like" or "what my community is like." And that we ask ourselves whether these organizations and all of our institutions have "this spirit of feeling love, of unanimity, of harmony, without rivalry or conceit." Do they exist "with humility" and do we "think that others are superior to us?" Is "this spirit" truly there or is there perhaps "something to improve?" So, he said, it's good to ask ourselves "today, how can I improve this?" And to follow St. Paul's advice, "in order that the bishop's joy may be complete; in order that Jesus' joy may be complete."

God's Gift Is Free

November 4, 2014
PHIL 2:5-11; LK 14:15-24

We shouldn't be afraid of the gratuitousness of God which upsets the order of human convenience and exchange. Pope Francis highlighted this idea during his homily at St. Martha's on Tuesday, November 4. His reflection was inspired by a passage from the gospel of Luke (14:15-24), which follows the one in which Jesus explained that in God's law, "quid pro quo doesn't work," and in order to make the concept understandable, he advised: "when you give a feast, invite the poor, the maimed, the lame, the blind, and you will be blessed, because they cannot repay you. You will be repaid at the resurrection of the just."

"When one of those who sat at the table" with Jesus exclaimed in response, "Blessed is he who shall eat bread in the kingdom of God!," in other words, "This would be wonderful!," Jesus replied with "the parable of the man who gave a great banquet" and whose invitation was rejected. The pope thus sought to explain the three responses given to the host by as many guests: "Everyone likes to go to a party, they like to be invited but there is something here that these three didn't like." The problem was: "invited to what?"

One in fact, boasting of having recently bought a field, sets his wish of "vanity," of "pride," of "power" first, preferring to go and check on his field, in order to "feel a little powerful" rather than "sitting as one of many at that lord's table." Another speaks about business—"I have bought five yoke of oxen and I'm going to examine them"—and thinks more about his earnings than of going "to waste time with those people," thinking: "they will discuss many things but I won't be at the center; I'll be one of many." Last is the man who offers the excuse of having just gotten married. He could also bring his wife to the banquet but he wants "the attention for himself." In this case, selfishness prevails. In the end, the pontiff underlined, "all three have a preference for themselves" and don't want "to share a party." Because, in reality, "they don't know what a party is."

The men in the parable—"who are examples of so many"—always show an "interest," they seek an "exchange," a "quid pro quo." The pope explained: "If I were the guest, for example, 'Come, I have two or three business friends coming from another country, we could do something together,' without a doubt no one would have excused himself." Indeed, "what frightens them is the gratuitousness," that "being one like the others." It is "selfishness," the desire "to be at the center of everything." When one lives in this dimension, when "one is self-centered," he ends up without horizons "because he himself is the horizon." And so it is "difficult to hear the voice of Jesus, the voice of God." And, Francis added, "behind this attitude," there is another thing, even "more profound": there is the "fear of gratuitousness." God's gratuitousness, in fact, compared with so many life experiences which have caused us to suffer, "is so great that it frightens us."

Man is disoriented. The pontiff recalled that this attitude is similar to that of the disciples on the road from Jerusalem to Emmaus. They said to each other, "We had hoped that he was the one to redeem Israel." And also, "the gift was so great that we were disappointed. And we are afraid." The same thing happened with the "most practical" Thomas, who said to those who spoke of the Risen Jesus: "Don't come with any stories," because "if I don't see, don't touch . . . I once believed, and everything collapsed! No. Never again!"

Even Thomas "was afraid of God's graciousness." In this regard, the pope recalled a popular saying: "When the offer is so great, even the holy are suspicious." In other words, when a gift is too large, it puts us on guard, because "graciousness is too much" for us. So, if "God offers us such a banquet" we think: "better not to get involved," better to be "with ourselves." We are indeed "more certain in our sins, within our limits," because nevertheless "we are at home."

On the other hand, to go out "from our home at God's invitation, to God's house, with the others," it "frightens" us. And "all of us Christians," the bishop of Rome admonished, "have this fear hidden inside," but not very much. Too often, in fact, we are Catholics but not too Catholic, "confident in the Lord, but not too much." And this "not too much," in the end, "diminishes" us.

Pope Francis then considered, in the gospel parable, the attitude of the host after the servant tells him of the guests' rejection. He is "angry, because he has been scorned." So he "sends him to bring all those who are outcast, the needy, the sick, through the streets and the lanes of the city; the poor, the maimed, the blind, the lame." And when the servant tells him there is still room in the hall, he tells him: "Go out to the highways and hedges, and compel people to come in," that my house may be filled. One verb, "compel them," which makes us think: "So many times," the pope highlighted, "the Lord has to do the same with us: with proof, so much proof," he "compels that heart, that spirit to believe that there is graciousness" in him, that his gift "is free, that salvation isn't bought: it is a great gift." God's love is, indeed, "the greatest gift."

Yet we, the pontiff concluded, are frightened and "we think that we can make holiness with things, and in the long run we become a little Pelagian." However, "salvation is free," even if we stubbornly argue, "I don't understand, Lord, tell me: this celebration for everyone, who pays for it? Do I have to pay for it?" We don't realize that, as Paul recalls in the letter to the Philippians (2:5-11), all of this "is free, because Jesus Christ, despite being in the form of God, did not retain the privilege, but 'emptied himself, taking on the form of a servant. He humbled himself.'" It is Jesus, the pope recalled, who "paid for the feast, with his humiliation to the point of death, death on the cross." This is the "great graciousness" of God.

"When we look at the crucifix, we say: 'This is the entrance to the celebration. Yes, Lord, I'm a sinner, I have many things, but I look at you and I go to the Father's feast. I trust. I won't be disappointed, because you have paid for everything.'" Thus "the church asks us not to fear the graciousness of God," because it can seem "folly." But Paul says: "Christ's cross is folly for the world; it cannot comprehend it. But it is he who has paid so that for us all it is free." We have only to "open our heart, do our part, all that we can; but he will provide the grand feast."

GOD ALWAYS GOES THE DISTANCE

November 6, 2014
PHIL 3:3-8A; LK 15:1-10

There cannot be Christians, much less pastors, who sadly stop "midstream" for fear of "getting their hands dirty" or of being gossiped about or of compromising their ecclesiastical career. It is God who demonstrates to each one of us and to the church as a whole the right manner of behavior, personally coming down "into the field" and always going "forward, all the way, always going out" with tenderness and with a single objective: "no one must be lost!," especially those who are distant. The pope gave this practical instruction during Mass at St. Martha's on Thursday morning.

Francis began with the day's gospel reading from Luke (15:1-10). He read that "the tax collectors and sinners were all drawing near" to Jesus "to hear him. And the Pharisees and scribes murmured, saying, 'This man receives sinners and eats with them.' They were scandalized." After all, the pope noted, Jesus' gesture "was a real scandal in that time, for those people, wasn't it?" To which he added: "Let's imagine that there were newspapers in that time." Perhaps the headlines would have read: "The prophet eats with these people!" In other words, it was a "scandal!"

Yet, Francis clarified, "Jesus had come in search of those who had distanced themselves from the Lord." And he made this easy to understand by telling "two parables: that of the shepherd," in order "to explain that he is the Good Shepherd; and that of the woman" who had ten coins and lost one. Analyzing the parables recounted by Luke, the pontiff highlighted that the words "most repeated in this passage are 'lose,' 'seek,' 'find,' 'joy,' and 'rejoice.'"

These very terms used by Jesus, the pope continued, "allow us to see what God's heart is like: God doesn't stop; God doesn't go only to a certain point" and stop. No, "God goes all the way, he goes the distance; he doesn't stop halfway to salvation, as if to say 'I've done it all, it's their problem!'" God instead "always moves, goes out, he takes the field." For example, the pontiff recalled a "particularly beautiful" phrase from the book of Exodus: "I have heard the cry of the Israelites who were enslaved by the Egyptians and I will go there." In other words, "God hears the cry and he goes: this is the Lord! This is his love: it goes the distance!"

In reality, Francis said, returning to the day's gospel passage, "Jesus is very generous because he almost compares these Pharisees and scribes with God," these people "who were murmuring." The parable begins with these words: "What man of you does not do this?" Perhaps it's true, everyone does it; however, they stop "halfway." Indeed, the pope indicated, "it was important to them that the balance of profits and losses was more or less favorable," and things were "going pretty well" with this way of looking at things. And thus, still looking to the two parables of Jesus in the passage from Luke, those tax collectors might have said, "yes, it's true, I lost three coins, but I earned so much!"

This kind of reasoning, however, "never enters God's mind!" Francis stated. Because "God isn't a businessman: God is Father and he always goes all the way; he goes the distance, to the end!" And this way—referring to another parable, that of the prodigal son—"even that poor elderly man who saw his son at a distance," even "he went all the way, as far as he could, that is, the roof of the house, to look every day to see whether his son had returned, for he didn't know where he was."

God does the same. "He always goes the distance. God is Father and this is God's love." This manner of God also tells "us pastors, us Christians" how to behave. It is really sad to see a pastor who stops "halfway; it's sad!" And he may even do something, but he explains that he can do nothing more. In fact, the pope remarked, "a pastor who opens the doors of the church and stays there, waiting, is sad." Just as sad is "a Christian who doesn't feel inside, in his heart, the need, the necessity to go and tell others that the Lord is good."

There is so much perversity, Francis said, "in the heart of those who see themselves as just, like those scribes, those Pharisees" whom Luke tells us about today. "They don't want to get their hands dirty with the sinners." And they say among themselves that if Jesus were a prophet, he would have known that the woman was a sinner. See "the contempt: they used the people, then they scorned them."

Thus, "being a halfway pastor is a failure." Indeed, "a pastor has to have the heart of God" in order to "go the distance." He has to have "the heart of Jesus, who had received that word from the Father: don't lose any one; don't lose a few; no one must be lost!" It is a matter which Jesus takes up again at the Last Supper, saying, "Watch over them, Father, that they not be lost!"

Thus, "the true pastor, the true Christian has this zeal inside; may no one lose it!" And "this is why he isn't afraid to get his hands dirty: he isn't afraid! He goes where he must go, he risks his life, he risks hunger, he risks losing his comforts, his status, even losing his ecclesiastical career. But he is a good pastor!"

And "Christians must also be this way." Because "it is so easy to condemn others, like the tax collectors did, but it isn't Christian! It isn't how children of God are! Indeed, "the child of God goes the distance; he gives his life, as Jesus gave his, for others." And thus, "one can't be calm, protecting oneself, one's comforts, one's reputation, one's peace of mind." This is why Francis firmly emphasized: "never halfway pastors! Never Christians in midstream!" We need instead to behave just as "Jesus did."

In this gospel passage, the pope continued, "it is said that these people were drawing near to Jesus," although "many times we read in the gospel that it is he who goes to seek people." Because of "the Good Shepherd, the good Christian goes out, is always outward bound: he always goes out of himself, is always going out toward God, in prayer, in adoration." And "he goes out toward others to bring the message of salvation."

Thus "the Good Shepherd and a good Christian embody tenderness." On the other hand, "those scribes, the Pharisees—

no, they don't know" what it means to take "the sheep onto their shoulders with tenderness, and carry it back to its place with the others." They are people who don't know what joy is. In fact, "a Christian and a pastor in midstream might know fun, tranquility, a kind of peace of mind." But "joy" is another thing, "that joy that is in heaven, that joy which comes from God, that joy that really comes from the heart of a father who goes to save" and says: "I have heard the cry of the Israelites and I have taken the field." Francis explicitly pointed out the beauty of "not being afraid that they speak ill of us" when we go "to find our brothers and sisters who are distant from the Lord." He concluded by asking the Lord for "this grace for each one of us and for our Mother, the Holy Church."

Two Coats of Paint

November 7, 2014
Phil 3:17–4:1; Lk 16:1-8

"Worldly Christians, Christians in name, with two or three Christian attributes but nothing more," are "pagans with two coats of paint." They seem to be Christians when we cross paths with them at Mass each Sunday; in reality they have slid gradually into the temptation of "mediocrity," such that they look "with pride and arrogance" at earthly things but not "at the cross of Christ." And it is this temptation that the pope warned about at morning Mass on Friday in the chapel at St. Martha's.

For his meditation, Francis recalled a passage from the letter of Paul to the Philippians (3:17–4:1), "his most beloved disciples," in which the apostle calls them "my brethren, whom I love and long for, my joy and crown." And he exhorts them to "imitate some but do not imitate others." In other words, he advises them "to watch those who behave according to the example you have in us: imitate these, the Christians who go forth in a life of faith, in a life of service, in the church. But do not imitate the others!"

It is easily understood from the text, the pope explained, that Paul had already spoken of this problem on various other occasions, because he adds, "I have often told you and now, with tears in my I eyes, I'll repeat it. Many live as enemies of the cross of Christ. Imitate these people, but not those people!" Yet, the pontiff continued, "both groups were in the church; all went together to Sunday Mass. They praised the Lord, they called themselves Christians and baptized their children." So, "what was the difference?"

Paul's recommendation to the Philippians is clear in this regard: "Do not even look at them! Why? Because they behave as enemies of the cross of Christ! Christian enemies of the cross of Christ!" In fact, the letter reads: "they glory in their shame, with minds set on earthly things."

In essence, Francis explained, they are "worldly Christians, Christians in name, with two or three Christian attributes, but nothing more." They are "pagan Christians." They have "a Christian name, but a pagan life" or, to put it another way, "pagans painted with two coats of Christianity: thus they appear as Christians, but they are pagans." The pope specified that "these people, our brothers," were not only in Paul's time. Today too, he advised, "there are many of them." This is why we "have to be careful not to slide toward that path of pagan Christians, Christians in appearance." In reality, "the temptation to adapt to mediocrity—the mediocrity of these Christians—is actually their downfall, because the heart cools; it becomes lukewarm." But "the Lord speaks a strong word to the lukewarm: 'because you are lukewarm, I will spew you out of my mouth.'" These people, the pontiff repeated, "are enemies of the cross of Christ. They take the name, but don't follow the requirements of Christian life."

Further examining the concept, "Paul explains this a bit and speaks about 'citizenship,'" underscoring that "our commonwealth is in heaven." However, the apostle indicates that the citizenship of the enemies of the cross is exclusively "earthly: they are citizens of the world, not of heaven." And their "surname is 'worldly.'" This is why Paul strongly advises: "Look out for them!"

Precisely because it is not an issue confined to the Philippians of Paul's time, the pope proposed a series of practical questions we should ask ourselves, for an examination of conscience: "At this point each of us—even me!—should ask ourselves: Do I have any of this? Do I have any worldliness in me? Something pagan? Do I like to boast? Do I like money? Do I like pride, arrogance? Where are my roots, that is, where is my citizenship? In heaven or on earth?" Do we belong to the earthly or the spiritual world? Indeed, Pope Francis explained, again quoting St. Paul, "our commonwealth is in heaven, and from it we await a savior, the Lord Jesus Christ." And that of the enemies of the cross? The apostle responds that "in the end their kind will meet with destruction." Thus, the pontiff emphasized, "these painted Christians will end up badly."

It's important, the pope continued, to look toward the end in order to see "where that citizenship that you have in your heart leads you": "worldly citizenship" leads "to ruin," whereas "that of the cross of Christ" leads "to the encounter with him," which is "so beautiful."

How do you realize that you are sliding toward worldliness, toward worldly citizenship? Francis highlighted that this is "a process that is done among us." It is "a temptation: one slides

toward worldliness." The signs to understand what we are moving toward, the pope said, "are in your heart: if you love and are
attached to money, to vanity and pride, you are on that bad path;
if you seek to love God, to serve others, if you are gentle, if you are
humble, if you serve others, you are on the good path." And thus,
"your identity card is good: it's from heaven." The other, however,
is "a citizenship that will bring you harm."

And Jesus beseeched the Father to save his disciples "from the
spirit of the world, from this worldliness, which leads to destruction." Then, in the letter to the Philippians, "Paul speaks of transfiguration." He writes: "Jesus Christ, who will change our lowly
body to be like his glorious body." And thus, those "who go on the
path of Jesus, in humility, in gentleness and in service to others, in
prayer, in adoration, will be transformed in glory. But the others
will also change." Paul "is clear" about this when he states: "Look
out for the spirit of worldliness." Because, the pope continued, "it
begins with little, but it goes slowly and is a journey that is made
without tiring."

It is like the day's reading from the gospel according to Luke
(16:1-8), which speaks of the steward. Francis asked, "How did
the steward get to the point of defrauding, stealing from his
lord? How did it happen," all in one day? "No! Bit by bit." Perhaps by "a tip here one day, a bribe there another day, and thus
corruption comes little by little." For "the path of the worldliness of these enemies of the cross of Christ is like this, it leads
you to corruption!" And then you "end up like this man, openly
stealing."

Hence "Paul's advice" to the Philippians: "Stand firm in the
Lord according to the example I have given you; and do not allow your heart and soul to weaken and end up in nothingness,
in corruption." This, the pope concluded, "is a beautiful grace to
ask for: to stand firm in the Lord. All of salvation is there; the
glorious transfiguration will be there. Everything will be!" Thus,

he reiterated, the grace to ask for today is that of standing "firm in the Lord and in the example of the cross of Christ: humility, poverty, gentleness, service to others, adoration, prayer."

SINFUL CHRISTIANS

November 10, 2014
TITUS 1:1-9; LK 17:1-6

"Sin, forgiveness, and faith" are three closely linked words that the pope put forth during Mass on Monday morning in the chapel of St. Martha's House. He extracted them from a passage of the gospel according to Luke (17:1-6), which speaks of these three very things. They "are three words of Jesus," Pope Francis pointed out, and "perhaps they weren't spoken together, at the same time, but the evangelist puts them together." And thus began the pontiff's reflection.

The first of the three terms underscored by the pope is "sin." "To me," he confided, "it is striking how Jesus concludes" his discourse: after speaking about sin he says, "Take heed to yourselves." Thus, he uses a "harsh" expression, asking them "not to sin." Luke writes that it is Jesus himself who says: "temptations to sin are sure to come"; but he also adds: "woe to him by whom they come!" And more precisely, "Woe to him who should cause one of these little ones, the people of God, to sin—the weak in faith, children, young people, the elderly who have lived a life of faith—woe to him who causes them to sin! It would be better to die!"

Jesus also addresses these particularly "harsh" words "to us, to Christians," and as a result "we have to ask ourselves: Do I sin?" And even before that, "what is sin?" The pope explained that sin "is to assert and profess a way of life—'I'm a Christian'—and then to live as a pagan who believes in nothing." And "this amounts to sin because it lacks testimony: faith confessed is life lived."

Along this line of reasoning Francis turned to the first reading, taken from the letter of Paul to Titus (1:1-9), highlighting that "Paul is writing to his disciple, Bishop Titus, and advises him how priests, bishops, as God's stewards, should behave." And "he gives other advice: that the priest—whether a priest or bishop—be blameless; not be arrogant, not look down on everyone; not be quick-tempered, but meek, not a drunkard, spiritual not irreverent; that he not be violent but peaceful; not greedy for gain, not attached to money, but hospitable, a lover of goodness, upright, just, holy, self-controlled, holding firm to the sure word as taught." For "when a priest—whether a priest or bishop—does not live like this, he sins, he causes scandal." And one is led to point out to him: "You, teacher, tell us one thing but do another!" And about this the pope stated: "The sins of priests do such harm to the people of God, so much harm! The church suffers so much because of this!"

These words are about priests but they also apply "to all Christians." It does not become "permissible to be arrogant, quick-tempered, a drunkard" simply by the fact that one isn't a priest. The words, therefore, are "for everyone," the pontiff remarked. One must realize that "when Christian men or women, who go to church, who go to a parish, do not live this way, they sin."

After all, Francis continued, we often hear "I don't go to church because it's better to be honest and stay home" than to be like those "who go to church and then do this, this, and that . . . " Thus we can see that "sin destroys, it destroys faith." And "this is why Jesus is so harsh" and repeats: "Take heed of yourselves, be careful!" This very exhortation of Jesus "will do us good to repeat today: Take heed of yourselves!" For "we are all capable of sinning."

The second word that Luke offers is "forgiveness." In the gospel, Jesus "speaks about forgiveness, and he advises us to never tire of forgiving: always forgive. Why? Because I have been forgiven." Indeed, "the first one forgiven in my life was me. And for this reason I have no right not to forgive: I am required, because of the forgiveness that I received, to forgive others." Thus, "forgive: one time, two, three, seventy times seven, always! Even in the same day!" And here, the pontiff clarified, Jesus "exaggerates in order to help us understand the importance of forgiveness." Because "a Christian who is incapable of forgiving sins: he isn't a Christian." This is why he tells them, "to frighten them a bit: if you cannot forgive, neither can you receive God's forgiveness." In other words, we "must forgive" because we have been "forgiven."

This truth "is in the Our Father: Jesus taught it there," the pope recalled. Of course, he acknowledged, the subject of forgiveness "isn't understood in human logic." In fact, "human logic leads you not to forgive, [but] to revenge; it leads you to hatred, to divisiveness." And thus we see "so many families divided" because they lack forgiveness, "so many families! Children distant from parents; a husband and wife drifted apart . . ." For this reason, "it is so important to think this: if I don't forgive, I don't have—it seems I won't have—the right to be forgiven, or I don't understand what it means that the Lord has forgiven me."

Of course, the pope stated, it's understandable why, on "hearing these things, the disciples said to the Lord: 'Increase our faith!'" Indeed, "without faith one cannot live without sinning and always forgiving." We truly need the "light of faith, that faith which we have received, the faith of a merciful Father, of a Son who gave his life for us, a Spirit who is inside us and helps us grow, the faith in the church, the faith in the baptized and holy people of God." And "this is a gift: faith is a gift." No one, Fran-

cis said, receives faith from books or by "going to conferences."
After all, precisely because "faith is a gift of God who comes to
you, the apostles said to Jesus: 'Increase our faith!'"

The pontiff concluded by suggesting an earnest reflection
on "these three words: sin, forgiveness, and faith." Regarding
sin, he recapped, it's enough to remember "only those words of
Jesus: 'Take heed to yourselves!' This is dangerous": better "to
be cast into the sea" than to sin. Regarding forgiveness, then,
the pope invited us to always remember that we were forgiven
first. And last, the aspect of faith, without which, he repeated,
"a life without sin and a life of forgiveness" could never be
possible

DON'T BE LAZY

November 11, 2014
TITUS 2:1-8, 11-14; LK 17:7-10

How should our faith be? This is the apostles' question and
ours as well. The answer is "a faith that is set within the
framework of service" to God and to our neighbor. A humble,
freely given and generous service which is always "complete."
Only in this way is it possible to truly open oneself to the hope of
the final encounter with Jesus. This was the Holy Father's reflection during Tuesday morning's Mass at St. Martha's.

Discussing the day's reading from the gospel according to
Luke (17:7-10), the pope referred back to a passage from the
previous day, in which the disciples request: "Lord, increase our
faith," to which Jesus responds, "If you had faith as a grain of
mustard seed, you could say to this sycamore tree, 'Be rooted up
and planted in the sea,' and it would obey you." Francis explained

that the Lord speaks of "a powerful faith," one strong enough "to work great wonders," but on one condition: that this be set "within the framework of service." It calls for complete service, such as that of the "servant who worked all day" and when he gets home "he must serve the Lord," prepare dinner for him, "and then relax."

It seems, the pontiff remarked, "somewhat demanding, a bit hard." One might advise "this servant to go to his union to seek some counsel" on how to deal "with a master like this." But what's asked for is "complete" service because it is the same that Jesus practiced: "He led the way with this conduct of service. He is the servant; he presents himself as the servant, the one who came to serve and not to be served."

When set on the "path of service," faith "will work miracles." On the hand, however, "a Christian who receives the gift of faith in baptism, but then does not take it forth on the path of service, becomes a Christian without strength, unfruitful, a Christian for himself, to serve himself, to benefit himself. Although this Christian may go to heaven," the pope said, "what a sad life!"

It happens, then, that "so many of the Lord's great things" are "wasted" because, as "the Lord clearly stated: service is exclusive," and one cannot serve two masters: God and wealth. In this regard the pontiff recalled "at the time of the prophet Elijah, the Israelites," who wanted to follow both Yahweh and Baal. Elijah said to them, "You are limping on both legs! Things cannot go on like this!" Because, Francis emphasized, "we need one Lord."

Pope Francis then went into the details of everyday life and the difficulties that a Christian has in putting the word of the gospel into practice. "We can distance ourselves from this conduct of service," he said, mostly out of "laziness." We become "comfortable, as did those five inattentive maidens who were waiting for their bridegroom but without having enough oil in their lamps." Laziness renders "the heart lukewarm." Thus, out of convenience we are led to seek justifications: "If this one comes, or if that one knocks at the door, tell them I'm not home, because they're coming to ask a favor, and no, I don't want . . . " In other words, laziness "distances us from service and leads to convenience, to selfishness." And, the pope commented, "so many Christians" are like this: "they are good, they go to Mass," but go "only so far" with regard to service. Yet, he underscored, "when I say service, I mean everything: service to God in adoration, in prayer, in praise," service "to our neighbor" and "service to the end." Jesus "is strong" about this and advises: "So you also, when you have done all that is commanded you, say, 'We are unworthy servants.'" It is important that service be "freely given, without asking anything" in return.

The pope continued to speak about another manner of moving away "from the conduct of service," which is that of "taking control of situations." This is what happened to the apostles too, who moved the people away "so as not to disturb Jesus," but in reality it was also for their own comfort: that is, "they took control of the Lord's time, they took control of the Lord's power: they wanted it for their little group." Actually, "they took control of this conduct of service, turning it into a framework of power." This is explained, said Francis, "when among themselves, they discussed who was the greatest"; and "it is understood when the mother of James and John went to ask the Lord that one of her sons be prime minister and the other the minister of the economy, with all the power in hand." The same thing happens to Christians who "rather than servants" become "masters—masters of the faith, masters of the kingdom, masters of salvation. This happens; it is a temptation for all Christians."

The Lord, however, speaks to us of serving "in humility," as did "he who, being God, humbled himself, lowered himself, debased himself: to serve. It is service in hope, and this is the joy of Christian service," which lives, as St. Paul writes to Titus: "awaiting our blessed hope, the appearing of the glory of our great God and Savior Jesus Christ." The Lord will "knock at the door" and "will come to find us" in that moment, the pope said, hoping, "Please, let him find us in this conduct of service."

Certainly, in life "we must really struggle against the temptations that seek to distance us" from this disposition, such as that of laziness, which "leads to convenience" and drives us to provide "incomplete service"; and the temptation to "take control of the situation," which "leads to arrogance, to pride, to mistreating people, to feeling important 'because I'm a Christian, I have salvation.'" The Lord, the pontiff concluded, "gives us these two great graces: humility in service, in order that we're able to say, 'we are unworthy servants,'" and "the hope in awaiting the appearing" of the Lord who "will come to find us."

IN THE KINGDOM OF GOD WITH 50 CENTS IN THEIR POCKET

November 13, 2014
TITUS 3:1-7; LK 17:11-19

The kingdom of God is already there in the everyday holiness lived unseen by those families who have only 50 cents in their pocket by month's end. But they don't give in to the temptation of thinking that the kingdom of God is merely a spectacle, like those who make a pageant of their wedding, turning it into a showplace for vanity and an opportunity to be seen. Pope Francis thus returned to the discussion of the commitment to living the faith with perseverance, from one day to the next, leaving room for the Holy Spirit in silence, in humility, and in adoration. He did so during Mass on Thursday morning in St. Martha's chapel, proposing the true characteristics of the kingdom of God.

The very fact that Jesus spoke so much about the kingdom of God made even the Pharisees "curious," such that, as seen in the day's Reading from the gospel of Luke (17:20-25), they ask him: "when is the kingdom of God coming?" To this question "Jesus responds quickly and clearly: the kingdom of God is not coming with signs to be observed; nor will they say, 'Lo, here it is!' or 'There!' for behold, the kingdom of God is in the midst of you.'"

Indeed, Francis pointed out, "when Jesus explained in the parables what the kingdom of God was like, he used calm, peaceful words," and he also used imagery to show "that the kingdom of God was hidden." Thus, Jesus compared the kingdom of God to "a merchant who looked here and there for fine pearls" or "another who searched for a treasure hidden in a field." Or he said that it is "like a net that gathers everyone or like a tiny mustard seed which would later become a large tree." Similarly, he also said, "the kingdom of God is like wheat: it is sown and you don't know how it grows" because "God grants the growth."

Jesus said that the kingdom of God is "always in silence, but also in struggle," explaining further that "the kingdom of God will grow like wheat, not surrounded by things of beauty but in the midst of weeds." But, Francis indicated, the kingdom is there. It doesn't attract attention; it is silent, quiet.

In other words, the pope said, "the kingdom of God is not a spectacle." So often, "the spectacle is a caricature of the kingdom of God." Indeed, we must never "forget that it was one of the three temptations." In the desert, Jesus was told: "go to the pinnacle of the temple and throw yourself down, and everyone will believe. Make a spectacle!" However, "the kingdom of God is silent, it grows within; the Holy Spirit makes it grow with our willingness, in our soil, which we must prepare." But it "grows slowly, silently."

The gospel of Luke recounts that Jesus renews his discourse, asking, "Do you want to see the kingdom of God?" And he explains: "They will say to you, 'Lo, there!' or 'Lo, here!' Do not go, do not follow them." Because "the kingdom of God will come like a flash of lightning, in an instant." Yes, Francis added, "it will manifest itself in an instant, it is within." However, he remarked, "I think about how many Christians prefer a spectacle to the silence of the kingdom of God."

In this regard, the pope recommended a brief examination of conscience to avoid falling into the temptation of the spectacle, by asking a few simple questions: "Are you a Christian? Yes! Do you believe in Jesus Christ? Yes! Do you believe in the sacraments? Yes! Do you believe that Jesus is there and that he has come here now? Yes, yes, yes!" Well then, Francis continued, "why don't you go to adore him, why don't you go to Mass, why don't you take communion, why don't you draw near to the Lord," so that his kingdom may "grow" within you? After all, the pontiff stated, "the Lord never says that the kingdom of God is a spectacle." Of course, he explained, "it is a celebration, but it's different! It's a beautiful celebration, a grand feast. And heaven will be a feast, but not a spectacle." Instead, "our human weakness prefers a spectacle."

This sometimes happens "in celebrating certain sacraments," he said, leading us to think about weddings in particular. We have to ask ourselves whether these people "have come to receive a sacrament, to have a feast like the one at Cana in Galilee, or have they come to have a pageant, to be looked at, out of vanity?" There is thus "a continuous temptation: not to accept that the kingdom of God is silent."

But, Jesus says in the gospel of Luke: "the day that noise will be made, as the lightning flashes and lights up the sky from one side to the other, so will the Son of Man be in his day, the day that noise will be made."

As opposed to a spectacle, the pontiff recalled, there is "the perseverance of so many Christians carrying the family forward: men, women who care for their children, take care of grandparents, who have only 50 cents in their pocket by month's end, but they pray." And the kingdom of God "is there, hidden in that holiness of daily life, that everyday holiness." Because "the kingdom of God is not far from us, it's close."

The very "closeness is one of the characteristics" of the kingdom. It is an "everyday" closeness. This is why "Jesus removes, from the minds of the disciples, the image of the kingdom of God as a spectacle." And instead, "when he wants to speak of the last days, when he will come in glory, the last day, he says: as the lightning flashes, so will the Son of Man be, but first he must suffer many things and be rejected by this generation."

Therefore, there is also suffering in the kingdom God. Take, for example, "the cross: the everyday cross of life, the cross of work, of the family," the cross of carrying on, and "this little everyday cross: rejection." Thus, "the kingdom of God is humble, like a seed: humble, but it becomes big by the power of the Holy Spirit." And we have to "let it grow within us, without boasting. May the Spirit come, change our soul, and lead us forth in silence, in peace, in quiet, in closeness to God, to others, in adoration of God, without pageantry."

Francis concluded with the invitation to ask "the Lord for this grace of caring for the kingdom of God that is within us and in the midst of us in our communities: caring with prayer, adoration, service in charity, silently."

Children's Day

November 14, 2014
2 Jn 1:3-9; Lk 17:26-37

Ascaled-down version of Youth Day in Rome, but even better—Children's Day, complete with a lively catechism lesson, up close and personal with the bishop of Rome. This was the experience had by a group of children from the parish of Santa Maria Madre della Providenza, who attended Mass at St. Martha's on Friday morning. Presiding at the Mass, Pope Francis said that in order "to pass the faith on" to kids today, we need people who don't just talk but "set an example."

Their presence at Mass didn't go unnoticed. "When I look to that side it seems like Youth Day!" the pontiff said at the start of his homily. He confided that, for him, it was like celebrating what they call "Children's Mass" in the parishes. "It's nice to see children," he remarked, because it's like "looking at the future, looking at a promise, looking at the world that's to come."

Then Francis began questioning the adults, the teachers: "What are we leaving the children? What example are we setting?" Most of all, referring to what had just been read from the second letter of St. John (1:3-9), he asked: "Do we teach what we heard in the first reading: to walk in love and in truth? Or do we teach them with words, but our life goes another way?" This is why the pope took care to repeat that "for us, watching children is a responsibility." In fact, "a Christian has to take care of kids, of children and pass on the faith, to pass on what they live, what's in his/her heart: we can't ignore the little plants that are growing."

For this very reason the pope recommended that "today it will do us good to consider what my attitude is with children, with teenagers, with young people." He proposed an examination of conscience by way of several questions: "What is my attitude like? Is it the attitude of a brother, father, mother, or sister who helps him/her grow, or is it an attitude of detachment?" Or do we have the attitude, he asked, that "they grow, I live my life . . . ?"

It's important to really recognize our conduct in this regard, he explained. Indeed, "all of us have a responsibility to give the best we have. And the best we have is the faith: give it to them but give it by example," not with words. "Words are useless. Today words are useless. In this world of the image, all of these [kids] have cell phones, and words are useless. What truly counts is setting an example." Therefore, the decisive question to ask ourselves about the education of the youngest is, "What do I give them?"

At this point, looking toward the pews where the children from the Roman parish were seated, the Holy Father turned directly to them, weaving a dialogue of questions and answers: "Why have you come to Mass? Do you know? Who dares to say it? Why have you come to Mass? Are you afraid to speak? Why? Don't be afraid!" And after greeting the parish priest, he again called on the children to answer out loud in response to his question about their attendance. "To see you!" said one boy, reading the minds of his friends. "To see me! Thank you, thank you so much!" the pope replied immediately, adding, "I like it! I like seeing you too! And what you said is important: to see a person, who is the bishop of the city, who is the pope, whom we see on TV, but whom we want to see up close." This, he indicated, is what the boy's answer, "to see you," really means.

However, he advised them, "it's also important that you are used to seeing adults, people who set a good example for you." That is, "to see the parish priest, priests, nuns at home, with the family: to see what they are like and how they live life, the Christian life."

Francis then returned to speaking with the children: "Have all of you made your First Communion? Yes? Everyone? And Confirmation? No one has made Confirmation?" Listening to the answers of each one, the pope commented, "You haven't made it? You haven't either? Who else hasn't made First Communion? You? Has anyone made Confirmation?" Among the kids present there were a few who were to receive the sacrament of Confirmation the very next week: "Now, so soon. Fantastic!" Francis encouraged them.

After all, he noted to his young interlocutors, "this is a path, a journey of Christian life that is beginning." And then he asked: "Which sacrament does Christian life begin with?" The response from the kids was immediate: "With baptism!" And the pontiff: "Good! With baptism the door to Christian life opens and then," as St. John said in the first reading: "Walk in truth and in love." This, Francis explained, "is Christian life: to believe the truth and to love, to love God and love others." Then, he pointed out, "First Communion is on this journey, Confirmation, marriage . . ." It is a "lifelong journey" and it is "important to know how to live it, to know how to live it like Jesus."

But the pope's questions didn't stop there. "In these sacraments, I'm asking you, is prayer a sacrament? No, prayer isn't a sacrament, but we have to pray." Continuing his lively conversation with the children, Francis then asked, "Don't you know how to pray? There, good: yes!" It's important "to pray to the Lord, pray to Jesus, pray to Our Lady, that they help us on this journey of truth and love."

He then resumed the initial thread which he had begun with the boy who confided having come to St. Martha's to see the pope. "You came to see me—which of you said this? You! It's true, but you also came to see Jesus, agreed? Or do we set Jesus aside?" And he added: "Now Jesus is coming to the altar and we will all see him: it's Jesus!" So, "in this moment we have to ask Jesus to teach us to walk in truth and in love. Shall we say it together? To walk in truth and in love." The pontiff wanted "only the kids" to repeat these words several times, with increasingly louder voices. Then, kidding them, he asked why they had been afraid to speak at first: perhaps because, seeing the time, they weren't "awake yet." Concluding, again along with the children, Francis asked "Jesus to give us this grace to walk in truth and in love."

CHRIST IN THE FACE OF THE OUTCAST

November 17, 2014
REV 1:1-4, 2:1-5; LK 18:35-41

A Christian is called to recognize the Lord in the outcast, without the airs of those—and there are so many even inside the Vatican—who feel "privileged" for being included in a "band of the chosen" and in that "ecclesiastical microclimate" which in reality distances the church from the people of God and the various peripheries. The pope said this on Monday morning during Mass at St. Martha's.

Francis referred to a passage from the gospel of Luke (18:35-43), indicating that "this gospel passage begins with an unseeing man, a blind man, and ends with him receiving his sight, and 'all the people, when they saw it, gave praise to God.'" There are "three categories of people in this passage: the blind man; those who were with Jesus; and the people," the pope explained.

The blind man, the pontiff continued, because of the "illness which took his sight, couldn't see; he was begging." And "perhaps he was often saddened" and wondered, "Why did this happen to me?" In other words, he was a man who "couldn't find a way out, an outcast." And thus "the blind man was sitting by the road-side" like "so many outcasts here" in the various streets and public squares of Rome. Today, the pope recalled, there are "so many, so many, sitting by the roadside."

That man couldn't see but "he wasn't foolish; he knew all that went on in the city." After all, "he was right at the en-trance to the city of Jericho" and thus, "he knew everything and he wanted to know everything." Such that "he heard the noise and inquired: what's happening?" In any event, Francis noted, he was "a man who found a way of life along this road, a beggar, an outcast, a blind man." However, "when he heard Jesus was coming, he cried out." And when "they told him to be silent, he cried out even louder." What was the reason for his behavior? The pope explained it this way: "This man wanted salvation, he wanted to be healed." And thus, the gos-pel reads: "Jesus said that he had faith." Indeed, Francis ex-plained, the blind man "gambled and won," even though "it's difficult to gamble when a person is so 'debased,' so marginal-ized." However, "he gambled" and he knocked "at the door of Jesus' heart."

The "second category of people" that we meet in the passage of the gospel of Luke is instead comprised of "those who walked with the Lord; they were walking ahead, leading the way." These were "the disciples, and the apostles too, those who followed him and went with the Lord." They were also "the converts, those who had accepted the kingdom of God" and who "were happy about this salvation."

This is exactly why "they rebuked the blind man to be silent," telling him, "Calm down, be polite! It's the Lord. Please, don't make a scene!" And in this way "they distanced the Lord" from the periphery. In fact, Francis stated, this peripheral man "was unable to reach the Lord, because this band—albeit with such good will—closed the door."

Unfortunately, the pontiff acknowledged, "this happens frequently among us believers: when we've found the Lord, without realizing, we create this ecclesiastical microclimate." And this is an attitude not only of priests and bishops, but also the faithful. It's a manner of conduct that leads us to say, "We are the ones who are with the Lord." However, it often happens that in "looking at the Lord" we end up "not seeing the Lord's needs: we don't see the Lord who is hungry, who is thirsty, who is in prison, who is in the hospital." Indeed, we fail to see the "Lord in the outcast" and this is "a very harmful climate."

The problem, the pope explained, is that "these people who were with Jesus had forgotten the harsh moments of their own marginalization; they had forgotten the moment and the place that Jesus called them." Therefore they said: "Now we are chosen, we're with the Lord." And they were happy with this "little world" but they wouldn't "allow people to disturb the Lord," to the point that "they didn't even allow children to approach, to draw near." Francis remarked that they were people who "had forgotten the journey that the Lord had made with them, the journey of conversion, of calling, of healing."

Recalling a passage from Revelation (1:1-5, 2:1-5), the pontiff described this as a reality that "the apostle John tells with a really beautiful phrase that we heard in the first reading: they had forgotten, they had abandoned their first love." And this "is a sign: in the church, the faithful, the ministers, become a group like this, not ecclesial but ecclesiastical"; when a group is privileged "with closeness to the Lord, there is the temptation of forgetting their first love." It is precisely "that beautiful love which we all had when the Lord called us, saved us, said to us, I love you so much." Even the disciples are tempted "to forget the first love, that is, to forget the peripheries, where I was before, even should I be ashamed of it." This attitude can be expressed this way: "Lord, this one has an odor, don't let him come to you." But the Lord's response is clear: "did you not have an odor when I kissed you?"

In facing the temptation of the "bands of the chosen," which are found in every age, the conduct of "Jesus in the church, in the history of the church," is described in this way by Luke: "Jesus stopped." This, the pope underscored, is "a grace. When Jesus stops and says, look over there, bring him to me," as he did with the blind man in Jericho. In this way the Lord "makes the disciples turn their heads to the suffering peripheries," as if to say, "Do not look only at me. Yes, you must see me, but not only me! See me in others too, in the needy."

Indeed, Francis indicated, "when God stops, he always does so with mercy and justice, but also, sometimes, he does so with anger." This happens when the Lord "is stopped by the ruling class" which he defines as the "evil and adulterous generation." Certainly, the pope commented, "this was no caress." Returning to the gospel and the episode of the blind man in Jericho, the pontiff wished to highlight that Jesus himself wants the man brought near and heals him, recognizing his faith: "your faith has made you well."

The third group presented by Luke is "the simple people who needed signs of salvation." The gospel passage reads, "all the people, when they saw it, gave praise to God." These people were, therefore, capable of "celebrating, of praising God, of losing time with the Lord." The pope also noted that "so often we find simple people, so many elderly women who walk, and sacrifice so much to go and pray at a shrine of Our Lady." They are people who "don't ask for privileges, they ask only for grace." They are "the faithful people who know how to follow the Lord without asking for any privileges."

So then, Francis summarized, the three categories of people who directly call upon us: "the outcast; the privileged, those who have been chosen and who are now subject to temptation; and the faithful people who follow the Lord to praise him because he is good and also to ask him for health, to ask him for so much grace."

This reflection, the pope suggested, should lead us to consider "the church, our church, which is sitting by this roadside in Jericho." Because "in the Bible, according to the fathers, Jericho is the symbol of sin." Thus, he urged, "let us consider the church watching Jesus pass, this outcast church." Let us consider "these nonbelievers, those who have sinned so much and who don't want to get up, because they don't have the strength to start over." And, the pontiff added, let us also consider the "church of the children, of the sick, of the imprisoned, the church of the simple people," asking the Lord "that all of us, that we have the grace of having been called" and that we "never, never, ever distance ourselves from this church. Let us never enter into this microclimate of privileged ecclesiastical disciples who distance themselves from the church of God that is suffering, that is asking for salvation, that is asking for faith, that is asking for the word of God." Lastly, the pope concluded, "let us ask for the grace to be faithful people of God, without asking the Lord for any privilege that may distance us from the people of God."

AM I ALIVE INSIDE?

November 18, 2014
REV 3:1-6, 14-22; LK 19:1-10

"The word of God can change everything" but we "don't always have the courage to believe" in it. During the Mass at St. Martha's on Tuesday, Pope Francis spoke about the "three calls to conversion" from the day's liturgy, explaining that "converting is not an act of will"; one doesn't think, "I'll convert now, it's convenient . . . ," or "I have to do it." No, conversion "is a grace." It's "a visit from God; it's the Son of Man who has come to seek and to save"; it's Jesus "who knocks at our door, at our heart, and says: 'Come.'"

What, then, are these three calls? The first is found in the book of Revelation (3:1-6, 14-22), where the Lord calls the Christians to convert because they have become "lukewarm." The pontiff explained that "Christianity, the spirituality of convenience, is neither too much nor too little." It is the attitude of those who say, "Don't worry. . . I'll do what I can; I'm at peace, and I don't want to be bothered with anything out of the ordinary." This is the case of those who feel comfortable and say: "I need nothing. I go to Mass on Sundays, I pray a few times, I feel fine, I'm 'in God's grace,' I'm rich, I'm enriched with grace, I don't need anything, I'm fine."

This frame of mind, Francis emphasized, "is a state of sin: spiritual convenience is a state of sin." And indeed, we read in Revelation: "For you say, I am rich, I have prospered, and I need nothing; not knowing that you are wretched, pitiable, poor, blind, and naked." The Lord does not mince words with "these comfortable Christians," to whom "he says everything to their face." We also read in the scripture, "because you are lukewarm, I will spew you out of my mouth." This expression, the pope noted, is "very harsh." At the same time, in order to help the Christians to convert, the Lord counsels them to clothe themselves, because "the comfortable Christians are naked." After a harsh word, the Lord then "draws a little closer and speaks with tenderness: 'so be zealous and repent.'" This, the pontiff said, is "the call to conversion: I'm at the door and I'm knocking.'" Thus, the Lord turns to the "faction of the comfortable, of the lukewarm" and calls on them to "convert from spiritual comfort, from this state of mediocrity."

There is then a second call, and this one is for those who "live for appearances." It is again Revelation which speaks of them: "you have the name of being alive, but you are dead." The Lord says to those who think they are alive, thanks only to appearance: "Awake," please, and "strengthen what remains and is on the point of death." Again, there is something living; strengthen it. And he adds tender advice: "Remember then what you received and heard; keep that, and repent. If you will not awake, I will come like a thief." The pope emphasized three words— "remember," "keep," and "awake"—imagining that this kind of man would think, "I appear to be Christian, but I'm dead inside." Appearances, Pope Francis said, "are the shroud of these Christians: they are dead." So the Lord "calls on them to repent: 'Remember, be awake, and go forward. There is still something alive in you: strengthen it.'"

Thus, we are all called to ask ourselves, "Am I one of these Christians of appearances? Am I alive inside? Do I have a spiritual life? Do I hear the Holy Spirit?" Do I listen to him? Conversely, beware of the temptation to say: "if all appears well, I have nothing to be blamed for: I have a good family, people cannot speak ill of me; I have all the necessities; I was married in church . . . I'm 'in God's grace,' I'm at peace." Look out, because "Christians of appearance . . . are dead." It is necessary, however, "to look for something alive inside and to strengthen it, by remembering and waking, so that it can go forward." It is necessary "to convert: from appearances to reality. From warmth to zeal."

Finally, there is the third call to conversion, that of Zacchaeus. Who was he? "He was a chief tax collector, and rich." He was a "corrupt man" who "worked for foreigners, for the Romans; he betrayed his homeland. He sought money in customs tariffs" and gave "part to the enemy of his homeland." In other words, he was "like so many leaders we know: corrupt"; people who, "instead of serving the people," exploit them "in order to serve themselves." Pope Francis indicated that Zacchaeus "wasn't lukewarm; he wasn't dead. He was in a state of putrefaction. Completely corrupt." Yet in front of Christ, "he feels something inside." He feels that "this healer, this prophet who they say speaks so well, I would like to see him, out of curiosity." Here we see the action of the Spirit: "the Holy Spirit is clever and has sown the seed of curiosity"; and in order to see Jesus, that man even did something "a little ridiculous": a leader, a "chief executive," actually climbed a tree "in order to watch a procession." How ridiculous "to behave this way." Yet he did, and "he wasn't ashamed." He was thinking, "I want to see him."

Inside this self-assured man, the pope explained, "the Holy Spirit was at work." And then it happened: "the Word of God entered that heart," with the Word, with joy. In fact, men who lived in "comfort" and men "of appearance had forgotten what joy was," while "this corrupt man received it straightaway."

The gospel of Luke recounts that he "climbed down in haste and received him joyfully," that is, he received "the Word of God, which was Jesus." And what happened "straightaway" to Zacchaeus is what had happened to Matthew (who was in the same profession): "the heart changed, he converted, and he gave his sincere word: 'Behold, Lord, the half of my goods I give to the poor; and if I have defrauded anyone of anything, I restore it fourfold.'" This, according to Francis, is an illuminating passage: "this is a golden rule. When conversion reaches your pockets, it's certain." He explained: "Christians at heart? Everyone. Christians in mind? Everyone." But, Pope Francis asked, how many are Christians when it comes to "our pockets? Few." Yet, conversion arrives "straightaway" before the "sincere word." By comparison, there is "the other word," that of those who don't want to convert: "when they saw it, they all murmured, 'He has gone in to be the guest of a man who is a sinner.' He has become soiled, he has lost purity. He must purify himself because he has entered the house of a sinner."

In conclusion, these are the three calls to conversion made "by Jesus himself": "to the lukewarm, the comfortable," and to those who are Christians in "appearance, those who believe they are rich but are poor"—indeed, "they have nothing, they are dead"—and last, to those "beyond death": the corrupt. Before them, "the Word of God can change everything. But the truth is we do not always have the courage to believe in the Word of God," to receive that "Word which heals us inside" and by which "the Lord knocks at the door of our heart."

This, Pope Francis concluded, is conversion, which "the church wants us to think very seriously about in these final weeks of the liturgical year" in order that "we may go forward on the path of our Christian life." For this we must "remember the Word of God," we must "safeguard it," "obey it," and "remain vigilant" in order to begin a "new, converted life."

The Fear of Surprise

November 20, 2014
Rev 5:1-10; Lk 19:41-44

Jesus often weeps for his church, even today, as he did before the closed gates of Jerusalem. At morning Mass at St. Martha's House on Thursday, Pope Francis spoke about the day's reading from the gospel of Luke, 19:41-44. He reminded us that Christians continue to close their doors to the Lord out of fear of his "surprises," which undermine established certainties and securities. In reality, he explained, "we are frightened of conversion because to convert means allowing the Lord to guide us."

The pontiff began his reflection with the image of Jesus weeping at the gates of Jerusalem. Jesus "wept over the city: he wept over her closure." He wept because the city was closed to him; she didn't want to receive him. Francis highlighted that this was similar to the apostle John weeping at the closed scroll, "sealed with seven seals," as told in the book of Revelation 5:1-10, which was heard in the day's first reading.

The pope remarked that this closing "makes Jesus weep; the closure of the heart of his chosen one, of his chosen city, of his chosen people," who "didn't have time to open the gate" because they were "too busy, too satisfied with themselves." Even today, "Jesus is still knocking on doors, as he knocked at the gate of the heart of Jerusalem: at the doors of his brothers, of his sisters; at our doors, at the doors of our heart, at the doors of his church." ⸱

The fact is, the pontiff explained, "Jerusalem was content, at peace with her life, and had no need of the Lord" and his salvation. This is why the city had "closed her heart before the Lord. And the Lord wept before Jerusalem. As he also wept at the closed grave of his friend Lazarus. Jerusalem was dead."

In weeping "over his chosen city," Jesus also weeps "over his church" and "over us." But why, the pope asked, "wouldn't Jerusalem receive the Lord? Because she was at peace with what she had, she didn't want problems." This is why Jesus exclaimed at the gates, "Would that even today you knew the things that make for peace! . . . because you did not know the time of your visitation." Indeed, the city "was afraid to be visited by the Lord; she was frightened of the gratuitousness of the Lord's visit. She was certain about the things she could manage."

This is an attitude seen among Christians even today, Francis noted. "We're sure about what we can manage. But the Lord's visit, his surprises, we aren't able to manage them. And Jerusalem was afraid of this: of being saved on the path of the Lord's surprises." The city was "frightened of the Lord, of her spouse, of her beloved." This was because "when the Lord visits his people, he brings us joy," but he also "brings us conversion. And we are all afraid." The pontiff emphasized that what we fear is not "happiness," but rather "the joy the Lord brings, because we can't control it."

In this regard, the pope recalled "Lamentations," which the choir sings on Holy Friday in the Liturgy of the Adoration of the Cross: "How lonely sits the city that was full of people! How like a widow, a solitary vassal has she become." The pontiff then recalled the Lord's dialogue with the city: "What have I done to you that you would respond this way?" and explained that the cross is "the price of that rejection." The cross is "the price to make us see the love of Jesus," that love which "led him to tears, to weep even today, so many times, for his church."

Jerusalem at that time "was at peace, content; the temple worked. The priests offered sacrifices; the people came in pilgrimage; the doctors of the law had everything organized": it was "all clear, all the commandments were clear." Nevertheless, the pontiff observed, "the gate was closed." He then invited an examination of conscience, starting with the question: "Today, we Christians, who know the faith, the catechism, who go to Mass every Sunday, we Christians, we pastors—are we pleased with ourselves?"

There is a risk of already feeling satisfied, because "we've got everything organized" and we don't feel the need for the Lord to make "new visits." But, Francis advised, Jesus "is still knocking at the door, of each of us and of his church, of the pastors of the church." And should "the door of our heart, of the church, of the pastors not open, the Lord weeps, even today," just as he did at the gates of Jerusalem, "lonely, once full of people, a widow." Jesus sees the city "and weeps because she doesn't open her gates, because she fears his surprises, because she is too satisfied with herself." Francis then concluded by asking us to consider: "How are we doing, at this moment, before God?"

THOSE WHO SCANDALIZE THE PEOPLE

November 21, 2014
REV 10:8-11; LK 19:45-48

Priests and lay people with pastoral responsibility must "keep the temple clean" and "welcome every person as Mary did," taking care not "to cause scandal for the people of God" and to avoid turning the church into a money exchange, "because salvation is free." This was the pope's recommendation on Friday morning, the Feast of the Presentation of the Blessed Virgin Mary, during Mass at St. Martha's.

Speaking from the day's reading taken from the gospel according to Luke, 19:45-48, Pope Francis said that in the temple, Jesus' act of "driving out the vendors" is actually "a ceremony of purification of the temple." The people of Israel "knew these ceremonies" because "they had to purify the temple after it had been profaned." Just think "of the reconstruction of the temple at the time of Nehemiah," the pope said. There was "always that zeal for the house of God, because the temple for them was 'the sacred,' and when it was desecrated it had to be purified."

Thus, "in this moment, Jesus is performing a purification ceremony," the pope repeated. He then confided: "I was thinking today about how this Jesus, zealous of the glory of God, with lash in hand, differs from the twelve-year-old Jesus who conversed with the elders. How much time has passed and how much has changed!" In fact, "Jesus, moved by zeal for the glory of the Father, performs this ceremony of purification—the temple had been desecrated"; not only the temple, however, but also "the people of God, who have been profaned by a sin so serious as scandal."

Referring again to the gospel, Francis remarked that "the people are good, they went to the temple; they weren't looking at these things. They were looking for God, they were praying." It was necessary, however, to "change currency in order to make the offering, and they did it there." It was actually to search for God that "the people of God went to the temple; not so for the vendors." From them "came the corruption that scandalized the people."

The pope recalled, in this regard, "a really beautiful scene of the Bible," which is also connected with the presentation of Mary. "When Samuel's mother went to the temple, she prayed for the grace of a son. She quietly whispered her prayers. The poor, old, but very corrupt priest" called her "a drunkard." At that time, "the priest's two sons exploited the people, exploited the pilgrims, scandalized the people: the sin of scandal." The woman, however, "with such humility, instead of saying a few harsh words to this priest, explained her anguish." Thus, "in the midst of corruption, in that moment," there was "the holiness and humility of the people of God."

Let's consider, the pontiff continued, "those people who were watching Jesus clean house with a lash. Luke writes: "all the people hung on his words." In light of this gesture of Jesus, "I think of the scandal that we can cause for people with our conduct, with our unpriestly habits in the temple: the scandal of trade, the scandal of worldliness." Indeed, "how often, even today, do we see, as we enter a church, there's a price list: baptism, so much; blessing, so much, Mass intentions, so much . . . " People are scandalized by this.

The pope also told about an event that he experienced personally. "Once, newly ordained, I was with a group from the university and a couple who wanted to get married." They went to a parish to arrange the wedding Mass. "And the parish secretary there said: No, no, you can't." And they asked why they couldn't have a wedding Mass, since a Mass was always recommended in order to marry. "No, it's not possible, because you can't take more than twenty minutes." Why? "Because there are time slots—But we want a Mass!—Then pay for two slots!" So, "in order to marry with a Mass they had to pay twice." This, the pope said, "is a scandal." And we know "what Jesus says to those who cause scandal: it would be better to be cast into the sea."

It's a fact: "when those who are in the temple—whether priests, lay people, secretaries who manage pastoral care in the temple—become profiteers, the people will be scandalized." And all of us, the laity as well, are responsible for this. Because, Francis explained, "if I see this going on in my parish, I have to have the courage to speak to the priest's face," otherwise, "the people suffer that scandal." And it's curious, the pope added, that "the people of God lose their priests when they have a weakness, slipping on a sin." However, "there are two things that the people of God cannot forgive: a priest attached to money and a priest who mistreats people." The scandal of a "house of God" that becomes a "house of trade" is hard to forgive. This is exactly what happened with regard to "that wedding: the church was for rent" in shifts.

In the gospel Luke doesn't say that "Jesus is angry," but rather that Jesus has "zeal for the house of God," which "is more than anger." But, the pontiff asked, "why does Jesus act this way? He had said and he expresses here: we cannot serve two masters. Either serve the living God or serve money." In this instance, "the house of the living God is a house of trade; the worship was actually of money." Jesus says instead, "It is written: 'My house shall be a house of prayer'; but you have made it a den of robbers." Thus, "He clearly distinguishes the two things."

But there is also another question: "why does Jesus have an issue with money?" Because, Francis answered, "redemption is free: God's graciousness." Indeed, Jesus "comes to bring us the full graciousness of the love of God." This is why, "when the church or the churches become profiteers, it's said that salvation isn't so free." It is for this very reason that "Jesus takes the lash in hand to do this rite of purification in the temple."

The liturgical Feast of the Presentation of Mary in the Temple reminds the pontiff of a prayer. Recalling that the Virgin enters the temple as a "simple woman," Francis hoped that this would "teach all of us, all priests, all those who have pastoral responsibility—to keep the temple clean" and to "lovingly welcome those who come, as Our Lady did."

WHERE THE LIGHT COMES FROM

November 24, 2014
REV 14:1-3, 4B-5; LK 21:1-4

In the widow who places her two coins in the temple treasury, we see the "image of the church" which must be poor, humble, and faithful. For his homily during Mass at St. Martha's on Monday morning, Pope Francis drew his reflection from the gospel according to Luke, 21:1-4. He referenced the passage in which Jesus, "after long discussions" with the Sadducees and the disciples about the Pharisees and the scribes who, "pleased with having the first places, the first seats in the synagogue," look up and "see the widow." There is an immediate and distinct contrast between her and "the rich putting their gifts into the treasury of the temple." And the widow is actually "the strongest person here, in this passage."

And twice this passage says that the widow "is poor: two times. And that she is in poverty." It's as if the Lord wanted to highlight to the doctors of the law: "you have such a wealth of vanity, of appearance, and even of arrogance. This one is poor. You, who devour the widows' livelihoods . . . " In the Bible, however, "the orphan and the widow are the most marginalized figures," as are the lepers, and this is why "there are so many commandments to help, to take care of widows and orphans." Jesus "looks at this lonely woman, simply dressed," who gives "all that she has to live on: two coins." We also think of the widow of Zarephath, "who welcomed the prophet Elijah and before dying gave all that she had: a handful of meal and a little oil . . . "

The pontiff recreated the scene of the gospel narrative: "a poor woman in the midst of the powerful, in the midst of the doctors, the priests, the scribes . . . also in the midst of those rich men giving their offerings, a few even doing so to show off." Jesus says, "This is the journey. This is the example. This is the path you must take. This one." Like the "gesture of this woman who was all for God, like the widow Anna who welcomed Jesus in the temple: all for God. Her hope was in the Lord alone."

Francis stated that "the Lord highlighted the figure of the widow." The pontiff, in fact, is fond of seeing "in this woman an image of the church." First, the "poor church, for the church needs to have no riches other than her Spouse"; then the "humble church, as the widows were in that time, for in that time there was no pension, there was no social welfare . . . nothing." In a certain sense the church is "a widow somewhat, because she is waiting for her Bridegroom to return . . . " Of course, "she has her Spouse in the Eucharist, in the Word of God, in the poor, but she is waiting for him to return."

What of "the figure of the church can be seen in this woman?" Francis pointed to the fact that "she wasn't important"; her name didn't appear in the newspapers, "no one knew her. She had no

degree . . . nothing. Nothing. She did not shine of her own light."
Likewise, the "great virtue of the church" is not "shining of her
own light," but rather reflecting "the light that comes from her
Spouse." Especially since "over the centuries, when the church
wanted to have her own light, she was wrong." Even "the first
fathers" said that the church is "a mystery like that of the moon.
They called her mysterium lunae," indeed, because "the moon
doesn't have its own light" but instead "receives it from the sun."

Of course, the pope explained, "it's true that sometimes the
Lord may call on his church" to have "a little of her own light."
We remember when he asked "the widow Judith to take off her
widow's garments and array herself in her gayest apparel to do a
mission." But, the pontiff said, "her widow's attitude continued"
to direct her "toward her Spouse, toward the Lord." The church
"receives light from there, from the Lord," and "all the services we
do" in the church help her "to receive that light." When a service
is lacking this light, "it's not good" because "it causes the church
to become rich, or powerful, or to seek power, or to lose her way,
as has happened so many times in history," and, Pope Francis
pointed out, as it happens "in our life when we want to have another light—our own light, which is not really that of the Lord."

The gospel, the pope noted, presents the image of the widow in
that precise moment in which "Jesus begins to sense the resistance
of the ruling class of his people: the Sadducees, the Pharisees, the
scribes, the doctors of the law." It's as if he were to say, "All this
happens, but look there!" Look at that widow. The comparison is
crucial in order to recognize the true reality of the church which,
"when she is faithful to hope and to her Spouse, is joyous at receiving light from him, of being, in this sense, a widow: waiting
for that Sun to come."

After all, "it's not surprising that the first harsh encounter that
Jesus has in Nazareth, after the one he had with Satan, occurred
because he mentioned a widow and he mentioned a leper: two

outcasts." There were so many widows in Israel at that time, "but only Elijah was invited by that widow in Zarephath. And they got angry and wanted to kill him."

When the church is humble and poor, Francis concluded, and even "when the church confesses her misfortunes—we all have them—the church is faithful." It's as if the church were saying: "I am darkened, but light comes to me from there!" and this "does us so much good." Thus, "let us pray to this widow who is surely in heaven" that "she may teach us to be this kind of church," renouncing "all we have" and keeping "nothing for ourselves" but instead giving "all for the Lord and for our neighbor." Always humble and "without boasting of having our own light," but "always seeking the light which comes from the Lord."

Depression or Hope?

November 27, 2014
Rev 18:1-2, 21-23, 19:1-3, 9; Lk 21:20-28

Francis called for hope, that we not become depressed and frightened by a reality filled with so many wars and so much suffering. He reminded us that great buildings constructed without God are destined to collapse, such as it was for "wicked Babylon," which fell due to the corruption of spiritual worldliness. So it was, too, for the "distracted Jerusalem," which fell because it was self-sufficient and incapable of welcoming the Lord's visitations. And this is why the right Christian attitude is always "hope" and never "depression." This was the essence of Pope Francis' words during morning Mass on Thursday in the chapel at St. Martha's. He dedicated the celebration to the Blessed Virgin of the Miraculous Medal, who is dear to the spirituality of the Daughters of

Charity of St. Vincent de Paul, the congregation which provides services at St. Martha's Guest House.

"In these final days of the liturgical year," Francis pointed out, "the church proposes that we meditate on the end, on the final days, on the end of the world." And she does this through "various images, different topics," and tomorrow's will be "signs of the times." She "again draws our attention toward the end: the appearance of this world will melt away and there will be another earth, another sky; but this one will end; it will end up transformed." Thus, he explained, the church calls us today to reflect on "the figure of two cities, the collapse of two cities: two cities that didn't listen to the Lord, that fell away from the Lord; two cities that felt self-satisfied." And thus, in the first reading from Revelation (18:1-2, 21-23; 19:1-3, 9), John speaks about the fall of Babylon, while in the gospel reading, Luke (21:20-28) recalls Jesus' words regarding the fall of Jerusalem.

However, Francis explained, "the fall of these two cities happens for different reasons." On one hand is Babylon, "the symbol of evil, of sin." It is read in Revelation that Babylon had become "a haunt for demons, a cage for every unclean spirit, a cage for every unclean and disgusting beast." Babylon fell because of its corruption. The apostle calls Babylon the "great harlot who corrupted the earth with her harlotry." Babylon, Francis stated, "was corrupt, felt itself to be the master of the world and of itself, with the power of sin." And "when sin accumulates, the capacity to cope is lost, and decay begins."

But "it happens this way with people too, with corrupt people who don't have the strength to cope." The pope explained that "corruption gives you a sort of happiness, it gives you power and it also makes you feel self-satisfied"; however, "it doesn't leave room for the Lord, for conversion." This is also true of a "corrupt city." The word "corruption" speaks of many things today: of "not only economic corruption, but corruption with so many different sins;

corruption with that pagan spirit, with that worldly spirit." After all, the pontiff remarked, "the worst kind of corruption is the spirit of worldliness." Jesus, in fact, "asked the Father to protect his disciples from the world, from the spirit of the world, which makes you feel as if you're in heaven here," enjoying abundance. However, "inside, that corrupt culture is a putrefied culture: dead and worse . . . This cannot be seen."

Hence, Babylon is the "symbol," the pontiff said, of "every society, every culture, every person separated from God," and also of those who are "separated from the love of neighbors" and who, in the end, "decay within themselves." And thus, "this Babylon, which was a haunt for evil ones, fell due to its spirit of worldliness, it fell due to corruption; she separated from the Lord because of corruption."

On the other hand, Pope Francis stated, "Jerusalem fell for another reason." First of all, "Jerusalem was the bride, the betrothed of the Lord: He really loved her!" However, "she wasn't aware of the Lord's visitations" and she "made the Lord weep," to the point that he said: "How often would I have protected you as a hen with her brood: you were unaware of my visits, of the many times that God visited you."

Therefore, the pope indicated, "Babylon fell because of corruption; Jerusalem fell because of distraction, for not welcoming the Lord who came to save her." Basically, Jerusalem "didn't feel the need to be saved. She had the writings of the Prophets, of Moses, and that was enough for her." The writings, however, were "closed." As a result, there was "no room left to be saved, the door was closed to the Lord." And thus, "the Lord knocked at the door, but there was no one available to receive him, to hear him, to let him save them." And in the end, Jerusalem fell.

The pope advised that "these two examples can make us think about our life. We too, one day, will hear the blast of the trumpet." But "which city will we be in that day? In the corrupt and sufficient Babylon? In Jerusalem, distracted and with closed doors?" In any case, in the end, both will be destroyed.

In this period, however, "the message of the church doesn't end with destruction. In both texts there is a promise of hope." Indeed, in the moment in which Babylon falls, "the cry of victory is heard: Alleluia! Blessed are those who have been called to the wedding feast of the Lamb. Alleluia, now the wedding feast begins, now that all is clean!" Babylon, the pontiff added, "wasn't worthy of this feast."

With respect to the fall of Jerusalem, the text "comforts us greatly with these words of Jesus: 'Raise your heads!'" The Lord calls us to "look" and not become "frightened by the pagans," since "the pagans have their time and we must bear it with patience, as the Lord withstood his passion." This is why the Lord says to "raise your heads!"

The pope concluded his meditation with this call to hope: "When we think about the end, the end of our life, the end of the world, every one of us will have our end; when we think about the end, with all our sins, with all our history, let's think of the feast we will be given gratuitously and let's raise our heads." Therefore, let there be "not depression" but "hope." It's true, Francis acknowledged, that "reality is grim. There are so many, many populations, cities and people, so many people who are suffering; so many wars, so much hate, so much envy, so much spiritual worldliness and so much corruption." This is why, the pontiff confirmed, we have to ask "the Lord for the grace to be prepared for the feast that awaits us, with our heads always high."

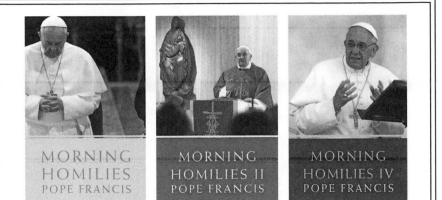